Searching

FOR

Meaning

ISBN: 978-1-950791-21-7

Cover and text layout design: Kristi Yoder

Printed in the USA

Published by:
TGS International
P.O. Box 355
Berlin, Ohio 44610 USA
Phone: 330.893.4828
Fax: 330.893.2305
www.tgsinternational.com

Searching for Meaning

A Study of Ecclesiastes

Lester Bauman

Table of Contents

Introduction

Did you ever get lost? Perhaps you were separated from your parents in a strange place, like a large department store. Do you remember that first flash of horrified realization when you looked around and your parents were gone? And how you felt sicker and sicker as you scanned the faces of the crowds of shoppers around you and couldn't find even one familiar or friendly face?

One of my daughter's first grade students crept into a culvert-like hole during a game of hide-and-seek and got stuck there. After a frantic search my daughter finally found the little tyke but couldn't get him out. It took the whole teaching staff around twenty minutes to set him free. The poor child was brave until he was released. Then, through his tears, he told my daughter, "I thought I would never see my family again."

Adults sometimes have those experiences too. Though adults

normally don't get too upset or afraid by being separated in a department store, I once experienced it during a time of depression in my life. I couldn't find my wife, and a flash of sheer terror ripped through me, almost incapacitating me. Losing your friends or your family is one thing, but even worse is realizing in a moment of introspection that you have lost touch with God and He feels strangely remote and unreal. Or worse yet, He is nowhere to be found and you need Him desperately—*right now.*

I suspect this is what happened to Solomon, the man who has traditionally been named as the author of Ecclesiastes. In it, we find Solomon's description of how he tried to find his way back. Hopefully, if you are facing a similar dilemma, it will help you find your way back as well. Or maybe it will help you to not lose track of God in the first place.

Either way is okay, but finding your way back can be a long, drawn-out process that doesn't always end well. It is better to avoid the wrong path in the first place.

A Note on Understanding Ecclesiastes

It is hard, at times, for people to understand the ancient Middle Eastern way of thinking. This is especially true if we were raised under the modern Western compulsion for detailed accuracy and structure in writing. It is difficult to fit most Biblical books into a structured outline because the writers didn't think in the logically organized ways we are accustomed to.

To understand the Bible properly, we need to read it from the writer's perspective as much as possible. This is especially true of books like Revelation, Song of Solomon, and Ecclesiastes. All three of these books are filled with word pictures, and you will not get very far with them if you insist on a literal interpretation of their words. Solomon knew that some of the things he said in Ecclesiastes weren't literally true. The Middle Eastern mindset wasn't concerned about that. Solomon often exaggerated and used strong terms in his writing. He painted his "word pictures" with a broad brush and in vivid colors, with the intent of speaking through impressions. He didn't tell lies—he painted word pictures. To the Middle Eastern mentality, the two ideas weren't even related. Jesus used similar methods in His parables and other teachings.

Along with this, Solomon used a semi-scientific method to explore his ideas. Mostly, he used observable data on which to build his arguments. He didn't quote other Scripture, and he didn't appeal to God to support his thinking. He often started out with a thesis statement or question, then explored its implications like a modern philosopher might.

This is a unique way for a book in the Bible to be written, but an interesting one. It is also a method that reveals a lot about Solomon's thought patterns.

Note that I am not a Greek or Hebrew scholar, nor a theologian. As an alternative, I normally approach a Bible study by reading the text in question in various translations normally considered trustworthy. The Bible is its own best commentary, and the best method of interpretation is to "compare Scripture with Scripture." I will refer to some of these comparisons throughout the book, although the main quotations are from the King James Version.

PART ONE

Vanity— Examples of Disillusionment

I read a quote recently that said, "The more intelligent you are, the less likely it is that you will believe in God." (My paraphrase.)

Solomon was very intelligent, and intelligent people sometimes use their intelligence in a wrong way. Doing so can lead to skepticism, and that seemed to be Solomon's viewpoint. But as we will see, this viewpoint leads to a lot of difficulties.

The first two chapters of Ecclesiastes describe this viewpoint.

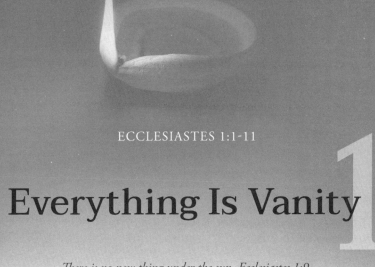

Everything Is Vanity

1

There is no new thing under the sun. Ecclesiastes 1:9

Prelude

Every "thinker" needs a sanctuary—a quiet haven with no distractions to disturb one's thought processes. Here is how I envision Solomon's:

Solomon's "thinking room" was a little cubicle he would have called his study, had there been such a thing in his time. It was little more than a cell furnished with a writing table, a chair, and some rudimentary writing materials. His working area was lit by several oil lamps since he did most of his reading and writing either late at night or early in the morning.

¹⁸And it shall be, when he sitteth upon the throne of his kingdom, that he shall write him a copy of this law in a book out of that which is before the priests the Levites: ¹⁹And it shall be with him, and he shall read therein all the days of his life: that he may learn to fear the lord his God, to keep all the words of this law and these statutes, to do them: ²⁰That his heart be not lifted up above his brethren, and that he turn not aside from the commandment, to the right hand, or to the left: to the end that he may prolong his days in his kingdom, he, and his children, in the midst of Israel. Deuteronomy 17:18-20

One wall had a window of sorts, facing west. Mostly it was just a hole in the wall, with shutters that he could close if the breeze was too cold or the sun too bright. But it was big enough that he could see out without standing up.

The door in the sidewall opened into his sleeping quarters and was the only way to enter the room. The room was heated through the door by the fireplace in the next room.

The other two walls were the most important. They contained his library of scrolls, stored carefully on rough-hewn shelves. Some of the scrolls were obviously quite old and fragile. Others were newer, and several were written by Solomon himself. Many were copies of older clay tablets that Solomon's scribes had recopied onto parchment imported from Egypt. A few were even copies of oral traditions handed down from the unknown past which Solomon's men had tracked down. Perhaps the most important scrolls in the collection were the ones containing the Pentateuch, which Solomon had copied painstakingly in his own handwriting during the first years of his reign.

Solomon had just taken a scroll from his library and was looking through it. According to the title at the beginning of the scroll, it was a collection of wise sayings that he had been working on for years. Some of the sayings he had gleaned from his collection of other people's writings. Others were original with him. It contained, in a series of "snapshots," an overview of the wisdom of the wisest man who ever lived.

This scroll was an old friend of Solomon's. He often opened it when he was feeling pensive. Right now he was just starting on a new project—one that might prove to be his last—and he needed a springboard. Maybe he could find one in this collection of his thoughts from years gone by.

Of course, the above scene is my imagination. The process of writing in Solomon's time was much more difficult than it is today, and we don't know exactly what all was involved. We do know, however, that Solomon did a considerable amount of writing, so he had some means of getting his thoughts written down.

Vanity: Meaningless and Futile Nonsense (1:2)

The book of Ecclesiastes drips with frustration, especially in the first several chapters. Obviously, Solomon's sense of disillusionment had destroyed the zeal with which he had once approached life.

Solomon had an obsession, almost a paranoia, about everyday things that seemed useless, meaningless, or endless. In his opinion, anything without a rational reason for existing was an exercise in futility. We can see this in his descriptive word choices—using words like "vanity" and "vexation of spirit" to describe what most people just took for granted. A "vanity" is like the wispy, drifting fog on a cool morning in autumn. You can't get hold of it, and it seemingly serves no useful purpose. What could be more useless than a wispy patch of fog? Various times throughout Ecclesiastes, Solomon further described these "vanities" as being a "vexation of spirit." In other words, he found them irritating and frustrating.

The book of Ecclesiastes gives us an interesting glimpse into Solomon's mind and his frustrations and provides a key to understanding Solomon in his later years. He gradually—and maybe subconsciously—lost touch with God and the purpose in life that a relationship with God brings. More and more, he tried to find meaning in life by indulging in materialism, pleasure, sensuality, and philosophy. If we learn nothing else from the record of Solomon's life, we need to at least understand the futility of pursuing these to find meaning in life.

> [1]The words of the Preacher, the son of David, king in Jerusalem. [2]Vanity of vanities, saith the Preacher, vanity of vanities; all is vanity. (Eccles. 1:1, 2)

One thing seems clear: *Solomon was looking at death, and he didn't like what he saw.* Many of his questions make more sense if we approach them from that perspective. Life tends to look different when we get to the point that we realize not only that we *can* die or *might* die, but that we *will* die. I think that's where Solomon found himself. He could see death creeping up on him, and there was nothing he could do about it.

This realization provides the scenario for Ecclesiastes. It records the thoughts of a brilliant person trying to sort out what makes life worth living and doing so from a secular perspective. It appears he realized he was getting closer to death, and he desperately wanted to know the answers to his questions before he died. He didn't want to just sink into oblivion. He wanted to know that the world had changed because he lived, that those changes were worthwhile, and that he would be remembered for them.

Above all, Solomon wanted life to be fair and to make sense. He had little use for a God he didn't understand and who seemed unfair at times. Nor was there any use looking for meaning in life if things didn't make sense. But as Solomon eventually realized, life without God never makes sense. It never seems fair from our perspective. It is impossible to find meaning in life without first finding a relationship with God.

Solomon was an intelligent person. He wanted people and ideas and procedures to have a rational reason for existing. He wanted it all to fit together like a giant jigsaw puzzle. He knew it wouldn't be easy—big jigsaw puzzles seldom are—but he was the world's wisest man, and he thought it should be possible.

That is, if there weren't too many missing pieces.

Unfortunately, it seemed that the pieces he found didn't fit. It was as if someone had taken three or four separate puzzles and mixed the pieces together and then threw out half of them.

In the next sections, we will examine more closely some of the "vanities" that bothered Solomon. We will continue to follow these throughout the book because Solomon returns to most of them, sometimes more than once, in his search for missing pieces. Keep in mind that Solomon is speaking in pictures. Read the first eleven verses of this chapter and let the picture develop in your mind.

People Work but Nothing Changes (1:3)

Ecclesiastes 1:3 lists one of Solomon's major complaints with life. Seemingly, Solomon felt that life had cheated him. He had worked hard and seen other people working hard. But now it all seemed useless, because he could see that the money and possessions that came from working didn't bring happiness. When push came to shove, when he got desperate to find meaning in life, work was all for nothing. This meant that work was nothing but drudgery.

> What profit hath a man of all his labour which he taketh under the sun? (Eccles. 1:3)

We could argue with him about his conclusion. I can imagine one of his wives happening to read this verse in his notes. She could rightly have said, "Look at the temple you built for your God. That brought you a lot of satisfaction."

I wonder how he would have answered.

In a sense, Solomon's wife would have been right. I'm sure he had completed projects he felt good about. But Solomon seemed to be digging for something else. Getting up in the morning, working hard all day, and sleeping all night, only to do it all over again the next day and the next was a vicious circle. If you didn't get any benefit from it other than keeping you and your family alive, what was the use?

Solomon didn't seem to be able to put into words what he was looking for. What did he mean when he claimed that there was no "profit" in work? If profit was money, he had no right to complain. He was probably one of the richest people on earth, yet he seemed to lump himself with the poorest laborer in Jerusalem. He wasn't looking for money or simplistic answers. He was looking for that "magical" something that brought meaning to life.

And he could not find it. No matter how hard he tried, *he could not find it.*

Circuits: Cycles and Circles (1:4-7)

Solomon apparently had a fixation with circles and cycles of any sort. This was probably because they seemed to have no beginning and no end—no climax or fulfillment and no moment when the job was finally finished. He would have had no use for a number like zero, because it meant nothing. What could be more meaningless than a

⁴One generation passeth away, and another generation cometh: but the earth abideth for ever. ⁵The sun also ariseth, and the sun goeth down, and hasteth to his place where he arose. ⁶The wind goeth toward the south, and turneth about unto the north; it whirleth about continually, and the wind returneth again according to his circuits. ⁷All the rivers run into the sea; yet the sea is not full; unto the place from whence the rivers come, thither they return again. (Eccles. 1:4-7)

circle representing nothing?

The concept of zero is so simple that only a genius could have come up with it. Why do you need a symbol to represent nothing? Anyone acquainted at all with numbers and mathematics knows how important the number zero is. But Solomon's nature led him to look for complex concepts, and he seems to have overlooked the simple joys that life offered.

Solomon saw these circles everywhere. Generations came and went. People were born. They lived and died. They had children who did the same. It appeared like the earth would continue forever, and this endless cycle of meaninglessness would too.

And then there was the sun. It rose and set every day, just like clockwork, never missing a beat. The wind also traveled in cycles. Apparently Solomon knew about air currents and the water cycle, but in his eyes it was just another never-ending circle.

I'm not sure why Solomon didn't appreciate the marvels and order of creation, as he seems to have had an extraordinary knowledge of science for his time. But now he was blind to all that. He was caught in his own personal circle of pessimism and couldn't break loose. From his perspective, creation was stuck in one gigantic circle of meaningless cycles. Someone, once upon a time, had flipped a switch that started the universe in motion, then left it to its misery. Unless the universe malfunctioned or wore out, it would continue forever. It was a senseless, meaningless, perpetual-motion machine with no escape route but death.

Black Holes Are Never Filled (1:8)

Scientists have found spots in space they call black holes. The gravitational pull in these places is so strong that even light cannot escape from them. Anything that is caught in the gravitational pull of a black hole is sucked into it and compressed into an enormously dense mass.[1] Nothing escapes from a black hole. If it did, it would be totally unrecognizable after being crushed by immense gravitational pressures.

> All things are full of labour; man cannot utter it: the eye is not satisfied with seeing, nor the ear filled with hearing. (Eccles. 1:8)

Solomon would have sympathized with the concept of a black hole. It would have made a good illustration of what he saw happening around him. Work never ends or goes away. No matter how much work I do today, there is more for me to do tomorrow. The word *labor* in the KJV is often translated "weariness." Work drains your strength and makes you tired. Like a black hole, it seemed to him to have little value.

Solomon complained earlier that even though people die and new people are born, the earth keeps on forever. Work too keeps on forever. One man grows old and dies, but another man continues to do his work until he too dies and someone else takes it on.

Solomon saw no way to escape the endless cycle of work except by dying. Yet the thought of dying was not satisfactory either. A millennium or so later, Paul said, "For to me to live is Christ, and to die is gain." Solomon, on the other hand, felt that even though living was an endless cycle of meaninglessness and drudgery, dying was unthinkable because it was the end of everything he had lived for. The contrast between these two men is almost unfathomable.

Nothing Is New (1:9-11)

The book of Proverbs shows us that Solomon could be very practical when he chose. But in Ecclesiastes, he deals with pictures. What picture are you seeing in these first eleven verses?

Solomon is undoubtedly exaggerating for the sake of effect. He is deliberately painting a depressing, ugly picture, splashing his paint here

---

[1] The sun, for instance, might be compressed to the size of a pea, but the pea would weigh the same as the sun does in its uncompressed state.

and there like a five-year-old.

Why would he do this? Because to the natural man—the man without God—that is what life is like. He is going to enlarge on this further as we continue, but remember that. It is a key to understanding Solomon's pictures.

> ⁹The thing that hath been, it is that which shall be; and that which is done is that which shall be done: and there is no new thing under the sun. ¹⁰Is there anything whereof it may be said, See, this is new? It hath been already of old time, which was before us. ¹¹There is no remembrance of former things; neither shall there be any remembrance of things that are to come with those that shall come after. (Eccles. 1:9-11)

In this passage, Solomon points out the uselessness of creativity, something that he especially enjoyed. Do you want to write a book? So what? It's already been written by someone else, and he's done a better job at it than you ever could. Besides, that book has already been forgotten and so has its author. The same thing will happen to you. It's no use trying to create something new or beautiful. No one will appreciate it. You're just wasting your time. You're just a part of the meaningless cycle the universe is stuck in.

There is a common epitaph that reads, "Gone but not forgotten." That isn't true however. Most of us will be largely forgotten within a few years of our death. Solomon knew that, and he didn't like it. In a perfect world, life would make sense and death wouldn't destroy your reputation or people's memories of you. At least Solomon seemed to think so.

The idea of eternity doesn't show up much in Ecclesiastes, especially in the first part. Death was the end of almost everything in Solomon's estimation, or so it appears. This is probably part of the reason for his intense focus on trying to make sense of life. The person who has hope of eternal life doesn't need to worry about death as much. Death will be the last enemy we face and will seldom be easy. We don't normally look forward to dying. But if life is all we live for, then we will find ourselves fighting the same kind of pessimism Solomon struggled with.

Nathaniel Hawthorne wrote a short story about a young man who stopped at a small inn for the night and got to talking with the innkeeper about life. This young man was sure he was destined to become famous and would not die until his name was common household knowledge.

That night all the people in the inn were killed by a landslide. Hawthorne goes on to say that when people arrived the next morning and saw what had happened, they found some indication that there had been a guest at the inn that night. However, they couldn't be sure, and no one had any idea who the guest would have been. He commented on the young man's agony in dying. Not only was his desire for fame unfulfilled, but his very existence was in doubt. It was a terrible fate indeed for someone who pinned the meaning of life to popularity and being remembered after he died.

I think Solomon feared a similar fate. It would be the perfect finale for his first picture.

FOR DISCUSSION
Read Ecclesiastes 1:1-11
Note: Thinking through these questions will broaden the scope of your thinking. You should do this even if you aren't involved in a group discussion of the book.

Prelude
The chapter preludes are imaginary. The purpose of these preludes is to help us realize that Solomon was a real person, just like you and I are, with real problems, just like you and I have.

1. Does this prelude fit with what you know of Solomon? Why or why not?

Vanity: Meaningless and Futile Nonsense

2. Do you agree with the statement, "Solomon was looking at death, and he didn't like what he saw"? Explain your answer. How does facing death change our perspectives about life?

3. Think about the concepts of life being fair and life making

sense. In what ways are they necessary if we are to find meaning in life? In what ways can we find meaning even if life isn't fair and doesn't seem to make sense?

People Work but Nothing Changes

4. How does "work" illustrate Solomon's phobia about life being meaningless?

Circuits: Cycles and Circles

5. List some of the cycles that you see in life. How might these depress you? How might they do the opposite?

6. How did the cycles Solomon saw feed his phobia that life was meaningless?

7. Think of the idea of the universe being a "senseless, meaningless, perpetual-motion machine with no escape route but death." What modern-day philosophies mirror this kind of thinking?

Black Holes Are Never Filled

8. How does satisfaction in life help people find meaning in life? In what way doesn't it?

Nothing Is New

9. Is creativity useless? In what ways do you agree with Solomon's sentiments? In what ways do you think he is wrong?

10. Think of this statement: "If life is all we live for, then we will find ourselves fighting the same kind of pessimism Solomon struggled with." Why is this true?

The Vanity of Seeking Knowledge

The fear of the LORD is the beginning of knowledge: but fools despise wisdom and instruction. Proverbs 1:7

Prelude

Solomon was thirsty for knowledge, especially in his younger years. That was one reason he spent so many mornings or evenings in his thinking room. Here he could put aside the cares of being a king and think about the deep things in life. Much of the book of Proverbs had come out of this room.

But during the last few years, something had changed. He now spent more time watching the setting sun through the window than he did reading and writing. Somehow, some of the joy had gone out of his intellectual pursuits. He wasn't sure why, but it wasn't the same anymore.

Tonight it was evident that the king was depressed. It seemed like all the big projects he had planned in this room were done, and nothing exciting was left. He had finished the temple. He had finished his palace. He had finished a house for his Egyptian wife. And, as his harem grew, he had finished a large women's quarters that now housed almost a thousand women.

Maybe Solomon had lost his interest in life because he had lost his enthu-siasm for living. Or maybe he had lost his enthusiasm for living because he had lost interest in life. He wasn't sure, but one thing he knew, life was dif-ferent than it used to be. At one time he could get excited about watching a flower go through its growth stages. He had loved nature and had sev-eral scrolls he had filled with his observations over the years. But all that had changed.

Tonight, for want of anything else to do, he was watching the sunset. And thinking about meaning in life. "Nature is beautiful," he mused. "But there must be more to life than beauty. Sunsets, storm clouds, blooming flowers . . . They are all beautiful in their own way, but that's all. Surely there's more to life than all these."

The "Wise" Man

What was Solomon famous for? The Queen of Sheba heard about him all the way down in Africa, and she made a long trip all the way to Jerusalem to see if the story was true. It would take over eight hun-dred hours to walk from Ethiopia to Jerusalem—probably about three months. I doubt if the Queen of Sheba traveled that far just to see Solomon's riches.

No, the Queen of Sheba wanted to see and hear Solomon's wisdom. She had a list of hard questions to ask him, and the Bible says that his answers, along with his wealth, took all the spirit out of her. She had expected that the stories she heard were exaggerated, but she concluded that she hadn't even heard the half of his greatness.

Solomon was aware of his wisdom and the way others felt about it. He mentions his wisdom in Ecclesiastes 1:16, along with his "great" experience of wisdom and knowledge. For some reason, he didn't acknowledge why he was so wise. Maybe at this point in his life he wasn't so eager to identify with the God he had turned his back on. Or maybe he thought the picture he wished to paint was more com-plete without God.

Anyway, Solomon decided to apply his greatest strength—his

wisdom—to this problem. The wisest man on earth should be able to decipher this puzzle. If there truly was meaning in life, he would be the person to find it. He would dig it up, one piece at a time, if necessary.

But he forgot one thing—some of the puzzle pieces were missing.

Solomon's Search

Solomon isn't clear about what he was looking for, or what he thought it would take to satisfy his obsession with discovering meaning in life. He complained in the first part of the chapter about the meaninglessness (vanity) of life, and here, in this passage, he mentions that he was seeking out everything that is done under heaven. Like a true scientist, he made a complete survey of the field he was going to study. I suspect he was still thinking in terms of finding meaning in life through work, even though he observed at the onset that the work God had given men to keep them busy was a "sore travail"—an "unhappy business," as the ESV translation says.

He really put himself into his project. He researched, he observed, and he analyzed. The "scientific method" Solomon used hasn't changed that much to this day.

Solomon seemed to suspect that "someone" had a master plan for the universe that went beyond the "irrational" orderliness in nature that troubled him. As a king, Solomon would never have undertaken a major building project or any other major undertaking without such a master plan. Surely whoever had fired up the universe had "embedded" something into the idea of work, or at least into life in general, to give it a reason for existing. At this point, he didn't acknowledge that this was God. But he did seem to believe that if he put enough brain power into his research and analysis, he'd be able to sort it all out and maybe even reproduce the missing "master plan."

Fatalism?

Solomon made an interesting observation in the middle of all this. He said, "That which is crooked cannot be made straight: and that which is wanting cannot be numbered." He felt that there were a lot of things wrong with life and a lot of missing pieces, but no one could change those things. Interestingly, he returns to this idea later in Ecclesiastes and comes to a different conclusion, but that is part of a different picture. In this picture, he portrayed an almost fatalistic viewpoint, picturing man and nature caught in the viselike grip of an unreasoning Fate.

Throughout the earlier part of the book, Solomon seems to feel that fate—or perhaps some indifferent Designer—had predestined the universe to a vicious existence with no escape. No escape but death, that is. He never says this exactly, but that is what seeps through the cracks.

Finally he bows to the inevitable conclusion. Wisdom is just vexation. The wiser you become, the more vexed you will be. The more he studied, the more convinced he was that the universe was badly crippled— and the more depressed he became at what he had learned.

Wisdom, Madness, and Folly

Really, how much difference is there between wisdom, madness, and folly? And who is wise enough to know which is which? Wisdom and folly will both drive you mad, so why bother with the work of becoming wise? Just sit back in your boat and relax. Why paddle upstream so desperately? Even if you paddle for all you are worth, you will still only slow down the progress of the boat. You are caught in the current and will inevitably go over the falls to your destruction. It's too bad that you know about them. You would enjoy the trip better if you didn't know.

So what kind of picture do you see by now? Some years ago, a man took a large bulldozer and effectively turned it into a tank. He covered it with two layers of heavy plate steel with concrete sandwiched between them. This was so effective that the local SWAT team couldn't penetrate it, not even with armor-piercing weapons. He sealed himself into the bulldozer and took it into town, where he started destroying buildings with it. The police tried desperately to stop him, but to no avail. Before it was over, he had done seven million dollars' worth of damage to various businesses, the town office, and the police station. They never did get him stopped—a building finally collapsed on him and he got stuck. Then his engine overheated and quit. He killed himself rather than give up.

Does that remind you of what Solomon was doing? He armed his mental "bulldozer" with all his "great experience of wisdom and knowledge." This was going to be another success story, only he got stuck, and there he sat—defeated and deflated.

Defeated and deflated. That's the idea we get from this picture. Our best efforts, using our greatest abilities, will not bring us meaning in life. If we leave God out of our personal picture, we will end up defeated and deflated.

Like Solomon.

You can apply many of Solomon's pictures to church life, as well as every other aspect of life. When church leaders push ahead without God, they will fail. Theological knowledge is not enough. Neither is experience in church administration, nor powerful leadership.

Many people seem to believe that if they can combine education (knowledge) with experience, it will give them wisdom. They can then auction themselves off to the highest corporate bidder in return for a six-figure salary. Many of these people will tell you that finding real meaning in life isn't that important to them. If they can enjoy life and find financial security, they are happy.

FOR DISCUSSION

Read Ecclesiastes 1:12-18

Prelude

The prelude suggests a relationship between having an interest in life and having enthusiasm for life. It seems evident from the earlier chapters in Ecclesiastes that Solomon had lost both.

1. Suggest some ways that a person might find life becoming drab and some reasons for it. Could Solomon have been experiencing a "middle-age crisis"?

2. Note the statement: "Much of the book of Proverbs had come out of this room." Why is it such a paradox that Proverbs and Ecclesiastes were written by the same author?

The "Wise" Man

3. Do you see any indications that Solomon was proud of his wisdom? If so, did this influence his life and writing?

Solomon's Search

4. What do you think Solomon was really looking for in this search? Did he understand what he was looking for?

5. Was it wrong for Solomon to look for meaning in life? What dangers do you see in this?

Fatalism

This is defined as the *belief that events fixed by fate are unchangeable by any type of human agency.* In other words, humans cannot alter their own fates or the fates of others.

6. It seems as if Solomon felt powerless, as if he were in the grip of an unsympathetic deity. Why do you think his search made him feel this way?

7. Why did his search depress him like this?

Wisdom, Madness, and Folly

Note the statement, "You are caught in the current and will inevitably go over the falls to your destruction." This continues the thought that you are caught in the hands of a force that makes you powerless.

8. Does knowledge always make a person miserable? Why or why not?

9. Must wisdom, madness, and folly go hand in hand?

10. Do you see any connection between this section and Proverbs 16:18?

The Vanity of Pleasure

3

And I will say to my soul, Soul, thou hast much goods laid up for many years; take thine ease, eat, drink, and be merry. Luke 12:19

Prelude

Naamah saw it all happen. She watched through the window from the women's quarters as her husband helped the Queen of Sheba descend from her litter. She noted the smiles they exchanged and the gracious way Solomon helped her alight.

"I wonder when he last looked at me like that." She didn't say the words out loud. But the wistful look on her face betrayed her thoughts.

She stepped back from the window to avoid being seen, though everyone within seeing distance was too occupied watching Solomon and the queen to notice anyone else.

"I wish he would never have become king. We were so happy when we first married." She thought back to when her son Rehoboam was born and the happy times they had as a little family. "I was an outsider, but no one cared back then."

She shook her head and stared moodily at the floor. "Everything changed when he became king. Suddenly I was just a 'commoner' and not quite good enough to be the king's wife. Even Bathsheba, his mother, changed at that point. She, of all people, should have known how I felt. She was an outsider too. But I suppose she had her own struggles.

"I remember when Solomon married that beautiful Egyptian princess. She was the first one . . . and I didn't see him as much after that. It seemed he forgot all about me, even though he assured me he still loved me and only married the princess for a political alliance. That was what he said, but it was what he did that hurt. All that time and money he spent to build her a fancy house. But me . . . I was just dumped in with the rest of his 'collection.'"

She watched Solomon and the queen walking to the palace. "How many women does he have by now? It must be hundreds." Her eyes narrowed and her lips quivered. She forced herself to turn away. "I might as well accept it. He hasn't changed yet."

Solomon used bright colors for this picture. He splashed colors in reckless abandonment, deliberately creating a chaotic picture. But while this painting will certainly attract your attention, it loses its attraction when you examine it as closely as Solomon did in this passage.

The picture Solomon painted has been a popular one throughout all ages. For obvious reasons. So what is this picture showing us?

Pleasure Without Law

God created pleasure. Pleasure is not sinful of itself, but pleasure without law is self-centered and seeks self-gratification at any cost. It doesn't matter who else suffers because of it—if I want it, I will have it. Solomon used the pronouns *I, me, my,* and *mine* forty-one times in this passage.[1] That focus on self is typical of pleasure-seeking, self-gratifying people.

---

[1] He used them 135 times in the entire book, so you have close to a third of the uses in these eleven verses.

In this passage, we see Solomon trying to find meaning in life by letting his passions have free reign. This has always been the nature of humans. Martin Luther once said, "He who loves not wine, women, and song remains a fool his whole life long." This thought is obnoxious to most Christian people, but it isn't as far removed from us as we might think. For us it might be "good food, romance novels, and contemporary music." Today, romance novels are giving way to "Christian" movies, and you might prefer classical music over contemporary music. But if we look for pleasure without being tempered by God's law, we are falling into the trap Solomon pictured in this passage.

We could insert a whole list of other things that tingle our senses and gratify our longings for pleasure.

As we read down over the list of the pleasures Solomon tried out, I don't think we would consider any of them necessarily wrong. In the right context and with the right motive, pleasure is proper. But pleasure does not give meaning to life—only God can do that. Pleasure enjoyed without

[1]I said in mine heart, Go to now, I will prove thee with mirth, therefore enjoy pleasure: and, behold, this also is vanity. [2]I said of laughter, It is mad: and of mirth, What doeth it? [3]I sought in mine heart to give myself unto wine, yet acquainting mine heart with wisdom; and to lay hold on folly, till I might see what was that good for the sons of men, which they should do under the heaven all the days of their life. [4]I made me great works; I builded me houses; I planted me vineyards: [5]I made me gardens and orchards, and I planted trees in them all kind of fruits: [6]I made me pools of water, to water therewith the wood that bringeth forth trees: [7]I got me servants and maidens, and had servants born in my house; also I had great possessions of great and small cattle above all that were in Jerusalem before me: [8]I gathered me also silver and gold, and the peculiar treasure of kings and of the provinces: I gat me men singers and women singers, and the delights of the sons of men, as musical instruments, and that of all sorts. [9]So I was great, and increased more than all that were before me in Jerusalem: also my wisdom remained with me. [10]And whatsoever mine eyes desired I kept not from them, I withheld not my heart from any joy; for my heart rejoiced in all my labour: and this was my portion of all my labour. [11]Then I looked on all the works that my hands had wrought, and on the labour that I had laboured to do: and, behold, all was vanity and vexation of spirit, and there was no profit under the sun. (Eccles. 2:1-11)

God's law is meaningless and will leave you feeling empty.

Excess is another factor that enters in here. If Solomon had listed one or two (or even three) of his "pleasures," we wouldn't think so much about it. But when you read this passage in one sitting, one of the main impressions you get is how many pleasures Solomon crowded into his life. He might be summarizing an entire decade of his life here. But still, he was really, *really* busy trying to gratify his desires.

The sad thing is that *it was all for nothing.* It was all meaningless. Empty. Useless.

Materialism Without God

In Solomon's painting, he listed his many possessions and material accomplishments with his pleasures. But I'd like to separate the two because pleasure bears the connotation of sensuality, while material possessions are somewhat different. We often define materialism as the desire to accumulate material goods—making it a synonym for greed or avarice. This is certainly one part of it, but I think Solomon went beyond that.

For him, the accumulation of wealth and possessions seemed to be almost an obsession—as if it were the one thing that would make life worthwhile. And in essence, if we hold anything higher than God, it becomes what we worship. This is probably the closest that Solomon came, in Ecclesiastes, to admitting his fall into idol worship. The worship of matter has been tied very closely to the worship of false gods during much of the world's history.

The hoarding of material possessions is a common temptation. Even young children try to keep other children from playing with their toys. Men don't like to loan out their tools or their motor homes. Women protect their prize dishes carefully and woe betide the child who drops one and breaks it. It's something we all have to deal with. The step from a possession to an idol is very small. Possessions are probably the world's major idols today, and electronic technology is adding dozens of items to the list of potential idols every year.

It might be worth listing some of Solomon's "great works" and some modern equivalents.

First, he lists houses, vineyards, gardens, orchards, and irrigation reservoirs. It reminds me of some of the large farming operations I have seen. It is common, for instance, for the farm owner and his family to live in what would be considered a mansion by over 75 percent of the world's population. Actually, most of us have a standard of living that only a small percentage of this world's people can match. Do we have idols? You decide. What is proper for one person may be an idol for someone else. But just because we can afford something doesn't make it right.

Solomon had slaves. But what about the brother who owns a large business and has a hundred employees? Solomon had great possessions of herds and flocks. He gathered silver and gold. How many Christians today have assets that would match or surpass Solomon's? He had men and women singers. What do we have? Could it be expensive stereos or home theaters? What about fancy pickup trucks? Or recreational vehicles?

Idols anyone? I don't want to advocate an extreme asceticism, because that can become idolatry as well. I am simply trying to awaken us to the fact that these things may be closer to home than we think. We will never find meaning in life through owning many and expensive possessions. If we are using possessions or activities to fill a void in our life, we are guilty.

Then I Considered . . .

Solomon gave his desires free reign. He collected everything that was "delightful" to men.[2] He designed a house of cedar for himself and a grand house for his Egyptian princess. He had parks and orchards

---

[2] Verse 8 of this passage contains a textual difficulty. The KJV translates the latter part of this verse as "I gat me men singers and women singers, and the delights of the sons of men, *as musical instruments, and that of all sorts.*" The italicized part of this verse certainly could fit the context as it stands. But the Hebrew in this passage is obscure, and most English versions translate it as "I got singers, both men and women, and many concubines, the delight of the sons of man," or something similar.

I prefer the latter rendering because it is the only place in Ecclesiastes where Solomon implies that women were a part of his downfall. It doesn't make sense for him to skip that during his introspection.

NOTE: Adam Clarke states that "For these seven words, there are only two in the original. These words are acknowledged on all hands to be utterly unknown, if not utterly inexplicable." He states that probably they refer to "wives and concubines; of the former of whom Solomon had seven hundred, and of the latter, three hundred; and if these be not spoken of here, they are not mentioned at all [in Ecclesiastes]." Note that he wrote this long before the modern translations that portray Solomon as speaking of his harem in this verse.

and man-made lakes. He worked *hard*. And he enjoyed his work and his pleasures and his possessions.

But one day he stopped to think about his accomplishments. One by one he listed them, examining each of them in minute detail. He thought of all the hard work that had gone into them and all the money they had cost him, and he realized that what he was really looking for—meaning in life—wasn't there. All his hard work, his grand projects, and his festive parties amounted to nothing.

He had become sidetracked.

Nathaniel Hawthorne wrote a fable about a scarecrow. A farmer dressed the scarecrow in a magnificent military uniform and put shiny boots on his feet, then set him up in a field of strawberries. The scarecrow looked down at his fancy clothing after the farmer went home, and his chest puffed out in pride. (Remember, I said it was a fable!) He decided to walk into town so people could admire his impressive clothing. He came to a house party hosted by the town's leading citizens and walked in. All the people flocked around him and told him how handsome he was. If it had taken place today, they would have taken selfies with him. It was a grand party while it lasted.

But the scarecrow happened to see himself in a mirror hanging on the wall. He was stuffed with straw. He had a carrot nose, two pebbles for eyes, and a broomstick for a backbone. He shrank in horror from his reflection. He fled from the house and ran for the "safety" of his field. He was just a scarecrow, no matter what other people said of him.

I think that somewhat describes what happened to Solomon when he got around to really looking at himself.

Remember, without God, you are only a scarecrow. Other scarecrows may flock around you and compliment you. They will especially enjoy the money you spend on them. Nothing is more riotous than a gathering of scarecrows, but that is not where you will find meaning in life.

FOR DISCUSSION

Read: Ecclesiastes 2:1-11

Prelude

We don't know much about Naamah. After all, she was only the first of a thousand women in Solomon's collection. We tend to read about all these wives without really thinking about the ramifications of a situation like this. Thinking about this will also help us understand Solomon a little better.

1. How do you think most of these women felt deep down in their hearts? Did they feel honored to be one of the king's wives or did they wish they could be living elsewhere? In short, how would *you* feel if you were in their shoes?

2. Considering your answers above, what does this tell us about Solomon?

Pleasure Without Law

People commonly have one of two responses to pleasure. Some say "if it feels good, do it," especially if it doesn't harm anyone else. Others try to avoid pleasure entirely since it seems to them a spiritual threat.

3. What are some practical ways that "pleasure without law" differs from pleasures enjoyed under God's control? What might make pleasure wrong?

4. Give some illustrations of "things that tingle (your) senses and gratify (your) longings for pleasure."

5. The last sentence in this section states that Solomon's search for pleasure *was all for nothing*. Why was this true?

Materialism Without God

6. A man once said, "Materialism is not when we have things, but when things have us." How do you see this portrayed in this passage?

7. Most of us live in a society that owns many things. How can

we decide when ownership becomes materialism and when possessions become idols?

Then I Considered . . .

8. Why might it be a good thing for you to list your accomplishments like Solomon did?

9. Take an honest look at yourself. In what ways are you like the scarecrow in Hawthorne's fable? What can you do about these areas in your life?

The Vanity of Good Works

4

*There is a way which seemeth right unto a man, but the end thereof
are the ways of death. Proverbs 14:12*

Prelude

*Solomon was standing in his thinking room, reading from a scroll of his
own writings. For some reason, he liked to stand while he was reading.
He could think more clearly on his feet, it seemed. And it gave him free-
dom to move around while he was thinking—which also helped his mind
to work better.*

*On the writing table in front of him were several sheets of rough papyrus.
They were scraps from finished scrolls, not sheets as we would picture them.
He wrote his thoughts on them and then had them transcribed onto finished scrolls. Normally his scribes would also copy several duplicates, which
were kept in a safe place in case the original was lost or destroyed. One copy
always went to the temple, where the priests kept a document repository of
all the holy scrolls and various other scrolls recording the history of Israel.*

The king was pondering a passage in the scroll he was holding. "There is a way which seemeth right unto a man, but the end thereof are the ways of death." He laid the scroll on the table and stroked his beard thoughtfully. "I think I remember writing that," he told himself. "But I don't remember if it was my own idea or if I found it in someone else's writings and liked it.

"Somehow life looks different in my old age than it did when I was younger. I had high ideals back then. Now I seem to have more questions than answers." He shook his head, thinking of the project lying partly finished on his writing table. He bit his lip as he remembered the message the prophet had brought him several years ago—a message that had shaken him to the core.

"Does God really care what men do? I used to think I knew Him. Now I'm not sure." He bit his lip again. "Maybe I was wrong. Maybe my wisdom isn't enough to see me through."

He glanced down at the scroll and reread the passage he had been looking at. "The end thereof are the ways of death."

He glanced thoughtfully out the window. "There must be a way to understand the maze of life—and God. I'll be dead soon enough, by all appearances. I don't have a lot of time left to figure it all out."

He picked up the scroll and returned it carefully to the shelf on the wall.

The Skeptic

Solomon portrayed life from a skeptic's perspective in this passage. So his painting was still discordant, and the colors clashed with each other. It was also drab and dreary, especially in comparison with the last one. But it was more realistic than any picture he had painted so far. He had put his self-indulgent inclinations behind him, apparently realizing the fallacy of trying to find God or meaning in life through worshiping pleasure or possessions. He had also calmed down and was taking a more contemplative look at life. He still couldn't understand why life—and therefore God—didn't seem fair, and he still reacted to that. But he was less emotional about it than he was in the first chapter of Ecclesiastes.

Solomon lists over thirty questions in Ecclesiastes. It is difficult to say which ones are hypothetical or rhetorical and which are actually close to his heart. But it seems that most of them represent genuine struggles he faced as he looked for meaning in life. However, his tone shifts throughout the book. At this point, he seems skeptical of almost everything around him. If you read Solomon's writings in Proverbs, you can see that he thinks very highly of wisdom. He almost places it on the same level as truth. In this passage, he seems to question if it is even worth considering.

Questions, however, can be good or bad. Many scientific discoveries have come about because someone asked a question. Many people have found their way to Christ because they asked questions about life. But questions can also be used to demean someone else's ideas, or to question the validity of a concept.

In this case, it seems Solomon was deliberately questioning something he believed in—that wisdom was worthwhile. Whether he did that for effect or whether he was genuinely skeptical, I'm not sure.

I don't think the book of Ecclesiastes was written in one sitting. Solomon obviously put a lot of thought into these sections. Sometimes he seemed to be emotionally involved, and his words almost shout at you when you read them. At other times he approached his subject more calmly and philosophically.

This was one of the latter times. It is interesting to see how he built his argument.

> ¹²And I turned myself to behold wisdom, and madness, and folly: for what can the man do that cometh after the king? even that which hath been already done. ¹³Then I saw that wisdom excelleth folly, as far as light excelleth darkness. ¹⁴The wise man's eyes are in his head; but the fool walketh in darkness: and I myself perceived also that one event happeneth to them all. ¹⁵Then said I in my heart, As it happeneth to the fool, so it happeneth even to me; and why was I then more wise? Then I said in my heart, that this also is vanity. ¹⁶For there is no remembrance of the wise more than of the fool for ever; seeing that which now is in the days to come shall all be forgotten. And how dieth the wise man? as the fool. ¹⁷Therefore I hated life; because the work that is wrought under the sun is grievous unto me: for all is vanity and vexation of spirit. (Eccles. 2:12-17)

The Philosopher

This was his question: Is it worth the effort it takes to become a wise person? Solomon had already done a lot of research into wisdom and written a lot of proverbs about it. In a sense, he was the world's expert about wisdom.

He approached the subject using a philosophical method. First, he admitted the superiority of wisdom over folly. He was almost forced to do this—after all, anyone who had read Proverbs knew this was what he believed. But that wasn't the question. He wanted to know if, in the long run, it was worth the effort to become wise. That's a totally different question, and it seems to indicate the depth of his skepticism at this point.

Solomon started his argument with a hypothetical and somewhat obscure illustration. I don't want to read too deeply between the lines, but I wonder if he was referring to his son taking over his kingdom. If so, he was evidently aware that Rehoboam was inclined toward folly and would probably do "mad" things because of this.

He also pulled an object lesson out of nature to help explain the difference between wisdom and folly. Light and darkness certainly made an apt parallel for his illustration. He went on to show that the wise man walked in the light because he had eyes in his head. He was sensible enough to watch where he was going and to plan his path. The fool, on the other hand, walked in darkness because he refused to open his eyes! Light was available for him, but he refused to see it. This is an exaggeration, of course, but it shows how he felt about Rehoboam, if that is who he was talking about. Even if he wasn't, it is still an interesting illustration of a foolish person stumbling his way along the path because he is too ignorant to open his eyes and see where he is going.

The Debater

Philosophically, this may have been interesting, but considering that his search was for God and meaning in life, it was pointless. However, he wasn't done yet. This was only his introduction. After painting a vivid picture of how intellectually superior the wise man was over the ignorant foolish man (who had probably landed headfirst in a mud hole by now), he finally got to the point he was trying to make.

What happens to the fool at the end of his life? *He dies and is forgotten.*

What happens to the wise man at the end of his life? *He dies and is forgotten.*

Now jump ahead a century. What is the difference now between the wise man and the fool? *Nothing.* And that is his point. What is the use of going to all the work of being a wise man when you end up exactly like the fool anyway?

Checkmate

You can almost hear a triumphant tone in his closing thoughts. In a hundred years, Solomon would be dead and gone, his body nothing but dust. And in a hundred years, the fool would be dead and gone as well. There was no difference. So obviously there is no lasting value in being wise. Case closed.

Solomon's conclusion was emphatic and left little room for his readers to disagree. "All is vanity and vexation of spirit." Or, as the NLT translation puts it, "Everything is meaningless—like chasing the wind." The evidence was in, and Solomon had drawn his conclusion: It is *not* worth the effort it takes to be a wise person.

What he said is true—*if you leave God out of the picture.*

Note that Solomon said nothing about life after death. We should always factor that into a discussion like this, but Solomon was reasoning from an agnostic's perspective. Thankfully, he returned to the subject later from a different perspective. We'll also return to it at that time. Even then, we may not totally agree with him, but we must keep in mind that Solomon is writing from a scientific, philosophical perspective. He is using mainly observable data and leaves life after death for other writers to pick up.

FOR DISCUSSION

Read Ecclesiastes 2:12-17

Prelude

The author of this book assumes that Solomon wrote Ecclesiastes late in his life and had written his proverbs earlier. Many of Solomon's proverbs address areas where he seems to have failed later in life.

1. First Kings 11 describes how Solomon shifted away from God in his older years. Could this happen to you? How?

2. Older people are often considered wiser because of their years of experience. In what ways could the opposite be true? Why?

The Skeptic

Most philosophical discussions begin with a question. Solomon asked various questions throughout Ecclesiastes. In this section, he seems to be asking, "Is it worth the effort to become a wise person?"

3. The author states that questions can be good or bad. What are several examples of each?

4. Are people always skeptics if they ask questions about things we believe to be unquestionable? Should we feel threatened by such questions? What attitude must influence any questions we ask?

The Philosopher

Many Christians don't think highly of philosophy and feel we really don't need it. Sometimes, however, honest questions can help us sort out our thoughts and gain new understanding.

5. Solomon made it clear that, intellectually, the wise person was superior to the foolish person. Why do you suppose this was an important part of his argument?

6. How do our worldview and our eternal perspective influence the kind of questions we ask?

7. Is it always wrong to exaggerate to make a point? Why or why not?

8. Look up the word "hyperbole" in a good dictionary. What are some figures of speech Jesus used that show a form of hyperbole?

The Debater

Solomon really shines at using rhetoric. He must have been an excellent debater in his time. This passage is more interesting for its illustration of Solomon's thinking and debating skills than it is for the conclusions he reaches.

9. In what ways was Solomon's conclusion right? In what ways was it wrong?

The Vanity of Working Hard 5

Surely every man walketh in a vain shew: surely they are disquieted in vain: he heapeth up riches, and knoweth not who shall gather them. Psalm 39:6

Prelude

Solomon was becoming increasingly anxious to finish his writing project. But he still had so many unanswered questions. He needed more time to think. Because of this he was spending a lot of time in his thinking room recently.

As was often the case recently, his thoughts focused on his past life. "I used to think I had all the answers," he mused. Almost sheepishly, Solomon reached for the scroll of his wise sayings. It seemed he spent more time reading his past writings than working on his newest project. "What have I lost that I had when I was younger?"

Sometimes his answers seemed tantalizingly close. But he just couldn't find the logic he needed to bridge that last gap. He had entered his search so confidently—secure in his wisdom. He had overcome every other hurdle in life. Surely his wisdom would see him through this one as well.

"But it hasn't." He tugged thoughtfully at his beard. "I must be growing

old. My thoughts don't come together like they used to."

He sat heavily in his chair, leaning his elbows on his writing table and propping up his chin with his hands. He shifted his weight uneasily. "Or is it just that I don't want to accept the answers anymore? Maybe I was wiser when I was young."

He got to his feet and started pacing the floor. "I wonder if the answer is so simple that I'm just looking past it . . ."

In this section, Solomon stated clearly for the first time why he hated work. Had he just figured it out, or had he been reluctant to admit it earlier? Or had he just been leading up to it? This section is also the first one where he mentioned God in a positive way. As we go through the rest of Ecclesiastes, we will notice that he continued to shift in that direction.

Because of this, the clarity of his picture improves somewhat in this section.

Did Solomon Really Hate Work?

Solomon had worked hard as a king. He had completed various important building projects. He had beautified Jerusalem and the surrounding area with his own private parks and gardens. And more importantly, he had made Israel economically successful beyond the wildest dreams of his forefathers. The Bible states that silver was of no account in those days, apparently because it was so common. There is no doubt that from a human standpoint, Solomon's work was successful.

It is obvious from other passages that Solomon had enjoyed his work when he was planning large building projects and lucrative economic ventures. He also enjoyed designing parks and gardens and orchards. He liked his work so much that he listed it along with his other pleasures in the first part of chapter 2. So what was his problem?

If you look closely at the passage we are considering here, you will notice that Solomon's problem with work wasn't that his accomplishments weren't worthwhile. No, he was troubled by the question of what would happen to his accomplishments after he died.

This startled me when it first became clear to me. A lot of what Solomon was unhappy with can be traced back to this idea. I spent some time thinking about this and wondering why Solomon was so paranoid about what would happen to the world after he died. He thought he saw a pattern in life that didn't make sense, and he didn't want his life to just blindly fade away and merge with meaninglessness.

It also seems as if Solomon wasn't convinced that his son had the ability to handle his wealth properly. Probably the foolishness that surfaced later in Rehoboam was already evident. Or maybe Solomon was just fretting about the fact that he would not be able to control what happened to his wealth and accomplishments after he was gone. His preoccupation with this seems rather selfish. "I worked for it, so I deserve to enjoy it myself!"

It could also be that he was reluctant to see the valuable resources he had worked so hard to put together be wasted by foolish mismanagement. Regardless of what his true thoughts actually were, I get the impression that Solomon simply threw his hands in the air and gave up.

Did Solomon Change His Mind?

I think Solomon was convinced that life should have meaning. But he expected this meaning to be something above and beyond the mundane experience of everyday life. He thought it should be something grand and wonderful, something that really jumped out at him when he looked for it. But it didn't work out that way.

Solomon approached his search from the perspective of an agnostic and a skeptic. This allowed him to rule out the idea that meaning is found in material things or in the pleasures of life. He depended a lot on his wisdom for this part of the search. Whether he did this deliberately, I don't know, but it shows us that man's wisdom and intellect are not sufficient to sort out the important questions of life.

At this point, Solomon seems to have given up that he would find

¹⁸Yea, I hated all my labour which I had taken under the sun: because I should leave it unto the man that shall be after me. ¹⁹And who knoweth whether he shall be a wise man or a fool? yet shall he have rule over all my labour wherein I have laboured, and wherein I have shewed myself wise under the sun. This is also vanity. ²⁰Therefore I went about to cause my heart to despair of all the labour which I took under the sun. ²¹For there is a man whose labour is in wisdom, and in knowledge, and in equity; yet to a man that hath not laboured therein shall he leave it for his portion. This also is vanity and a great evil. ²²For what hath man of all his labour, and of the vexation of his heart, wherein he hath laboured under the sun? ²³For all his days are sorrows, and his travail grief; yea, his heart taketh not rest in the night. This is also vanity. ²⁴There is nothing better for a man, than that he should eat and drink, and that he should make his soul enjoy good in his labour. This also I saw, that it was from the hand of God. ²⁵For who can eat, or who else can hasten hereunto, more than I? ²⁶For God giveth to a man that is good in his sight wisdom, and knowledge, and joy: but to the sinner he giveth travail, to gather and to heap up that he may give to him that is good before God. This also is vanity and vexation of spirit. (Eccles. 2:18-26)

an easy answer. He had nearly exhausted his options. The only thing left was to look back over his life again to see if he had missed something. Maybe the answer was back there somewhere, staring him right in the face.

In this passage Solomon finally recognized that life did have some joyous moments and that people did at times find enjoyment in work. First, however, he again points out the negatives. There is a lot of vanity in work; it fills your days with worries and can keep you awake at night. Then, perhaps almost reluctantly, he concedes that work does have value. It allows you to eat and drink and find enjoyment in a job well done.

I think he was deflated to discover that he might need to accept something as ordinary as this for the basic meaning in life. This was no flash-of-lightning breakthrough, no grand philosophical triumph to talk about with the Queen of Shebas of the world.

In Ecclesiastes 1:13 Solomon had mentioned somewhat sarcastically that the work God had given the children of man to do was an "unhappy business" (see ESV). In Ecclesiastes 2:24, he returns to the idea of God's involvement in life. He recognizes that the simple enjoyment of life is only possible because God has made it possible.

Searching for Meaning

But when he connects the dots and realizes that God could possibly favor those who please Him, he feels this is not fair. He goes so far as to imply that God somehow takes away what the sinner has accumulated and gives it to the righteous. I suspect that this verse reflects some wishful thinking. In fact, Solomon admitted as much in other parts of Ecclesiastes.

Fortunately, Solomon didn't stop there. While his basic conclusion at this point was true, it was still not the grand solution he had dreamed of. He must have known, when he stopped to think about it, that his conclusion in chapter two was incomplete. So the book doesn't end here.

FOR DISCUSSION

Read Ecclesiastes 2:18-26

Prelude

The prelude pictures Solomon thinking, "I wonder if the answer is so simple that I'm just looking past it . . ." Sometimes God lets us learn the hard way that our own answers don't work. Sometimes we need to let go and let God do the work for us.

1. Sometimes God wants us to wait for an answer. Other times He gives us one, but we don't recognize it. Or we may see His answer but reject it. How can we tell which is which?

Did Solomon Really Hate Work?

If you can measure success in dollars, Solomon was very successful. But financial success doesn't equate to satisfaction or to meaning in life.

2. What was Solomon's real problem with his work and accomplishments? Can you think of some solutions to his problem?

3. Solomon felt that life didn't make sense and wasn't fair. Why would this have made his struggles worse?

4. How would finding personal satisfaction in life have changed Solomon's viewpoint?

Did Solomon Change His Mind?

Solomon came up with somewhat of a solution in this passage, but I don't think it satisfied him. At least it didn't stop him from continuing his search.

5. Like Solomon, we tend to look for big answers or spectacular answers to our questions about life. How might this keep us from finding the right answers?

6. What answer did Solomon finally settle on? While this answer contains some truth, why wasn't it enough to make Solomon feel good about life? Why do you think he felt a need to include a caveat that sinners were excluded?

7. The author states that "his conclusion in chapter two was incomplete." Do you agree with that statement? Why or why not?

PART TWO

Facing the Realities of Life

The book of Ecclesiastes seems to have at least two turning points. The first two chapters dwell on the process of disillusionment. Chapters 3 to 7 are more philosophical in nature and more balanced. Solomon still spoke of being disillusioned with life, but he shifted from an agnostic, emotional viewpoint to a more intellectual, philosophical perspective. He examined time and work, then looked at the frailty of life. Then he switched to injustice, veered off to a warning about fearing God, and ended up with a lengthy treatise about the meaninglessness of wealth and human honor. In chapter 7, he veered off again to contrast wisdom and folly.

The Constraints of Time

6

Time is what we want most, but . . . what we use worst. —William Penn

Prelude

Solomon was sitting in his chair in his thinking room thinking about time. He wasn't quite sure why, but it might have been because one of his wives had died that week. He hadn't made it to her burial because he was entertaining a deputation from Egypt that day.

"So Hannah is gone." He leaned back and looked at the ceiling. "I remember marrying her. Sweet girl with lots of spunk. I thought for a while she'd be my favorite. But then another one came along."

He pulled at his beard. "What was that next one's name? Esther?" He couldn't remember for sure, but as far as he knew she still lived in the women's quarters. "She was my favorite too for a while."

"My wives are getting older." He bit his lip and drummed his fingers on the table in front of him. "It's strange how time has flown by. I've been king for almost thirty-eight years."

He leaned back in his chair again. "Hannah was almost ten years younger than I am. I wonder how much time I have left. I wonder if God has set a time for me."

It was an uncomfortable thought, and Solomon squirmed a bit. He preferred lofty philosophical thoughts. But he was wise enough to know that sometimes a person needed to be practical and face the inevitable.

Yes, his time was coming. Maybe that's why he was thinking about time.

At first glance Solomon appears to have taken up a completely different train of thought, going into chapter three. But I believe this passage is another one of the keys to understanding this book—some more pieces for his jigsaw puzzle. This picture shows us another perspective of what it means to be a human being.

I don't think Solomon just got carried away with a philosophical discussion about time and veered off his subject. He was still putting together his argument. It is entirely possible, and even quite likely, that he started this book with the ending already in mind. Every one of these pictures added something important to the overall portrait he was creating.

I mentioned before that Solomon doesn't speak of eternity. His observations were the kind that everyone could see and identify with. He didn't stray much beyond observable data to draw his conclusions, so he didn't speculate about life after death. Similarly, we will not realize how shackled we are by time until we get to eternity and the shackles fall off.

Time Adds Structure to Life

We are surrounded by time. Or, you might say, we are overwhelmed by time. In today's world, everything seems driven by time. We wake up in the morning to the beeping of an alarm clock and go to bed that evening when the clock tells us it's time to go. We don't just get up when we feel rested and go to bed when we feel tired.

Our work is regulated by time as well. We run out the door at 7:30 a.m. because we need to be at work by 8:00 a.m. We have a 15-minute coffee break at 10:00 a.m., a half-hour lunch break at noon, and another coffee break at 3:00 p.m. We then quit work at 5:00 p.m. and have supper at 6:00 p.m. Of course, this varies depending on our occupation. A farmer's schedule would certainly be different than that. His alarm clock may chase him out at 4:30 a.m., or even earlier, depending on the time of year and the area he lives in.

Even church starts at a certain time. Although churches normally don't ring a buzzer when it's time for the sermon to be over, most ministers know that if they go much past closing time, their audience will start to squirm and watch the clock.

Time has been with us since creation. In fact, human health and sanity both require the structure that time gives. God knew that we would need such a structure to exist and thrive.

Solomon disliked this structure. He felt trapped by the sheer repetitiveness of time. But God apparently was very careful in putting together the structure of time. The universe is so accurate and the structure of time so exact that man can predict eclipses and similar events centuries in advance. They can also place an exact date for such events in history if a writer mentions them. Any system as advanced and complex as the universe needs a very exact schedule or it will eventually self-destruct.

Time is an absolute. It is difficult for us to think of human existence in any other context. Structured people love time, and creative people may hate it. But we all deal with it.

At times, such as this passage, Solomon appeared to approach life from a fatalistic perspective. He seemed to think we are caught in a time-driven vortex over which we have no control. But in the broader context of this passage, he was referring to God's involvement in our lives. That is especially true of the passage that follows this one. So I tend to think he was laying the groundwork for a different perspective on his search for meaning in life. This picture isn't quite the same as the fatalistic or agnostic perspectives that he painted elsewhere.

This passage depicts a very structured view of life. The Hebrew word for "season," as it is used in 3:1, means "an appointed time."[1] This indicates a level of control from somewhere that we don't normally think of.

Time, in the end, is evidence of God's involvement in people's lives.

Time Adds Perspective to Life

In this passage, Solomon gave us a snapshot of human existence from a new perspective. Time is another cycle that binds us. It not only limits the length of our earthly existence, it also limits our perception of our existence. Time is a prison cell that locks us in and keeps us from seeing beyond our immediate surroundings.

Our horizons can become quite narrow sometimes, without us even realizing it. I spent two weeks in the hospital some time ago. The first two-thirds of that time, I was in a room where I couldn't see outside. I had walls on three sides and a curtain on the other side. I didn't realize how much this bothered me until they moved me to a different room. Now my bed was beside a window, and I could see out. I could see clouds and could look down into a little courtyard. I could see the sunshine, and I could watch it rain. It was wonderful, and it made me feel better almost immediately—just because my horizons had broadened.

My horizons still weren't that broad. The courtyard was surrounded by buildings,

[1]To everything there is a season, and a time to every purpose under the heaven: [2]A time to be born, and a time to die; a time to plant, and a time to pluck up that which is planted; [3]A time to kill, and a time to heal; a time to break down, and a time to build up; [4]A time to weep, and a time to laugh; a time to mourn, and a time to dance; [5]A time to cast away stones, and a time to gather stones together; a time to embrace, and a time to refrain from embracing; [6]A time to get, and a time to lose; a time to keep, and a time to cast away; [7]A time to rend, and a time to sew; a time to keep silence, and a time to speak; [8]A time to love, and a time to hate; a time of war, and a time of peace. (Eccles. 3:1-8)

---

[1] See Brown, Driver, Briggs Hebrew lexicon.

Searching for Meaning

and I was in the middle of a city. But it was better, much better, than being in a room where I couldn't see out. That is the difference perspective can make.

Time seems to be three-dimensional, yet it isn't. We often divide time into past, present, and future, which at first glance seems like three dimensions. But if we stop to think it through, that's not how it is. An old song says, "Yesterday's gone, and tomorrow may never come, but we have this moment today." Right now is the only time you have. You can't recapture yesterday or jump right into tomorrow. The only reality of time is today. In fact, if tomorrow comes, it will still be today.

Since you can't fast-forward time or rewind it, it is important to capture our moments as they flee past us. So how long does right now last? If God lays it on your heart to apologize to a friend for an unkind statement and he's standing beside you, you had better grab that moment, because once it's gone, it's gone. That moment will never come back, and who knows whether you'll have another opportunity to do it.

The box that time puts around us is very small. The dimensions of past and future are merely mirages that often fool us and tempt us to waste the only part of time we have any control over—today.

Time Is an Enigma

Men go to great efforts to explain human existence, as if understanding the realities of life would make them more bearable. In the first several chapters of Ecclesiastes, Solomon portrayed the universe as an uncaring and impersonal perpetual-motion machine. Once you were caught in its cogs, death was the only escape route. It's not an encouraging thought.

During the time frame that I am writing this, scientists and other "brilliant" people are toying with a similar idea of life and existence. They portray the universe as a complex mathematical model, running on some superintelligent extraterrestrial being's gigantic computer. Some are taking this idea so seriously that they are thinking of investing millions of dollars to help mankind escape the system. Like Solomon, they see the obvious design in the universe. And like him, they feel we are caught in a giant trap beyond our understanding or ability to control.

Maybe they should read the book of Ecclesiastes.

FOR DISCUSSION

Read Ecclesiastes 3:1-8

Prelude

Time will eventually catch up with all of us. I think it was this fact that motivated Solomon to write Ecclesiastes.

1. Many people try to ignore the passing of time. In fact, it sometimes seems as if people expect to live forever. How do you face the fact that time will run out for you someday?

Time Adds Structure to Life

This section states that "human health and sanity both require the structure that time gives."

2. Why do you think human beings require time to thrive, or even exist?

3. Various people have run experiments where people lived in caves with no access to time for a few months. Try to find some of these accounts and discuss what we can learn from them.

Time Adds Perspective to Life

Everyone has a perspective. A baby has a small perspective, while an astronaut may have a very large one. Normally our perspective grows with time and experience.

4. How is finding meaning in life affected by our perspective?

5. Could Solomon have enlarged his perspective? Would this have helped him find meaning in life?

6. Why did Solomon's spiritual perspective shrink as he grew older, rather than expand? What can you do to keep this from happening to you?

7. Why is it important to know that *now* is the only time you have, no matter how long you live?

Time Is an Enigma

When I was a teenager, people were discussing whether reality was real or just a mirage. Some intellectuals wondered if we were all just dreaming and would wake up to discover that reality is something entirely different. This seems ridiculous, but some of today's imaginings aren't any better.

8. Read the following passages and discuss the view of time that they give us: Psalm 103:15, 16; Job 14:1, 2; Isaiah 40:6–8; 1 Peter 1:24. What is a true understanding of life and time?

What About Eternity?

I resisted the temptation to add a section at the end of this chapter about eternity. Solomon didn't seem to want to talk about that in Ecclesiastes. But thinking of eternity helps us to realize that time is a temporary structure that God has put in place only for time. In eternity, things just are. There is no place for past or future tense. Nothing *was* or *will be*. It just is.

9. What differences will we see in eternity? Why do we have such a hard time describing these differences?

10. Discuss the repercussions of the fact that God is in eternity while we are in time, considering passages like 2 Peter 3:8.

Toil Is God's Gift to Men

7

*And all men shall fear, and shall declare the work of God; for they
shall wisely consider of his doing. Psalm 64:9*

Prelude

*Solomon loved beauty, but lately he had been too preoccupied to notice any
of the natural beauties of the Judean landscape surrounding Jerusalem. For
months, he hadn't even gone for a walk in his gardens or orchards. But
tonight he needed some time to think, so he decided to take a moonlit stroll
through the palace grounds before going to bed.*

*It had been a particularly trying day. "Being a king isn't what people
picture it to be," he thought. "There are so many responsibilities." Just that
morning he had needed to settle a boundary dispute between two important landowners, both of whom were sure that their neighbor had moved
the boundary between their holdings in his own favor. He had tried to
mediate the dispute fairly, but he sensed that neither man was happy with
the outcome.*

After that, the matron of the women's quarters came to him for help in settling a disagreement between the Egyptian princess and some of the younger concubines. The matron had tried to settle everyone down, but the Egyptian princess felt that since she had royal blood she had extra authority. Anyway, Solomon had ended up going to the women's quarters himself to calm things down. He had tried to pacify the princess and then reminded her and the rest of the women that the matron was in charge. But here again, no one had seemed very happy with his decisions. He could still see the hurt look in the princess' eyes. "Why can't they just live together in peace?" he wondered.

He pushed aside his memories of the day's events and stopped for a while to watch the moon rising over the Mount of Olives. "I should go on a walk like this more often," he thought. "This is like a balm for a troubled soul."

He remembered a song his father had written years ago and quoted the words softly, "When I consider thy heavens, the work of thy fingers, the moon and the stars, which thou hast ordained; What is man, that thou art mindful of him? and the son of man, that thou visitest him?"

The introductory scenario is imaginary of course. But Solomon could easily have written this section of Ecclesiastes after a day like the one pictured. In this section of Ecclesiastes, Solomon hit a balance between the tedium and stress of work and the beauty of creation. Sure, life can be tough, and often is. Work can be like that too, and we sometimes almost despair over it. But despite this, it is still possible to find beauty and fulfillment in a lifetime dominated by work.

Work Is Travail

Most people would agree with Solomon that work can be a travail, or as some translations say, a burden. We have a centerpiece on our dining room table that says, "All you need is warm socks, a good book, and a cup of tea." That, or something similar, is a dream for many people. Yet it has been proven over and over that such a life doesn't have meaning.

When a man retires and moves to the front porch to spend his days in a rocker, he disintegrates rapidly. Soon he is doing his relaxing in an old people's home or a hospital, and his daydreams center around the past when he was able to work.

Yes, work can be a burden and often is. But work adds meaning to life. It gives you a reason to get up in the morning. It takes you out the door (unless you work in a home office like I do). At work, you are somebody and you are needed. That is why it is so hard on our self-esteem and self-confidence when the boss comes along and tells us we aren't needed anymore.

Work does a lot more for us than give us the money we need to pay our expenses. Sometimes we get our eyes off the blessing and onto the burden. Then life becomes a travail. But it doesn't have to be that way.

Everything Is Beautiful

I recall driving home late one night after a hard day of teaching. At that point, my life was full of "travail," and it seemed like I could hardly handle it anymore. I was driving down a dark country road. It was a beautiful, clear night, and the stars were shining brightly. I pulled to the side of the road and wound my window down. I leaned back, positioned my head out the window, and watched the stars. As my eyes adjusted to the darkness, the stars shone brighter and brighter and I started to see details in the heavens that I didn't even know were there.

We spend so much of our time surrounded by light that we

> [9]What profit hath he that worketh in that wherein he laboureth? [10]I have seen the travail, which God hath given to the sons of men to be exercised in it. [11]He hath made every thing beautiful in his time: also he hath set the world in their heart, so that no man can find out the work that God maketh from the beginning to the end. [12]I know that there is no good in them, but for a man to rejoice, and to do good in his life. [13]And also that every man should eat and drink, and enjoy the good of all his labour, it is the gift of God. [14]I know that, whatsoever God doeth, it shall be for ever: nothing can be put to it, nor any thing taken from it: and God doeth it, that men should fear before him. [15]That which hath been is now; and that which is to be hath already been; and God requireth that which is past. (Eccles. 3:9-15)

seldom realize what beauties we miss in the darkness. But that night I just gazed at the sky and meditated. God had made all of this beauty and much more that I couldn't see with the naked eye. I'm not sure why He bothered, unless it was just that He could do it and wanted to show us a bit of His glory.

I sat there for at least fifteen minutes, forgetting everything else. When I finally pulled back on the road, I was refreshed. The day's "travail" had fallen away. I had a glimpse of God that night that I have never forgotten. Well, maybe I have at times, but every so often I remember. And it works its miracle in me anew.

One big difference between a man and an animal is the ability to appreciate beauty. We were created in the image of God. One of the attributes that God passed on to us is His appreciation of beauty. He built beauty into creation everywhere, then gave us the ability to appreciate it.

So if travail is overpowering you and life seems to be out of control, just step aside for a few moments. Look at the stars or admire the mountains or marvel at the beauty of a flower. And think about the God who took time to surround you with such beauty. Even Jesus did that. When the pressure became too great for the disciples, He told them to "come apart into a desert place and rest a while" (see Mark 6:31). Sometimes we need to do that.

The time of rest didn't last long for Jesus and the disciples. The crowds soon figured out where they went and followed them. But it was enough. It doesn't always take much, just enough to get reoriented and get our eyes on God.

Eternity in Our Hearts

Verse 11 of this passage, in the KJV, states that "He hath set the world in their heart." Most translations give this as "He has put eternity into man's heart," or something similar.[1] In the context of this passage, this seems to indicate that God placed within man an eternal perspective.

---

[1] Adam Clarke verifies the veracity of this translation.

This is what allows us to appreciate things like beauty, music, and love. It also enables us to understand abstract scenarios and logic, as well as giving us the ability to reason and be creative.

Our reasoning ability is limited, however, according to the rest of the verse. Solomon knew from personal experience that God hides some things from us. But the connection is there, providing a channel that God uses to communicate with us. This would include our conscience and our innate ability to tell right from wrong.

The "eternity" in our hearts also allows us to enjoy work that would be tedious if we didn't know what it will do for us. A horse can't reason through the idea of work in this way. It works because it must and has been taught to obey. It can't figure out that if it works hard, it will get a good meal at the end of the day. But a man can do that. Even a slave who has been treated like an animal all his life has that thread of reason within him that will spring to life if the right circumstances come along.

Eternity in our hearts is one of God's great gifts to us. Because of it we can enjoy life and do good. We can eat and drink and enjoy the fruit of our labor. We can love our wives and families. All of this should help us to find meaning in life.

But most of all, the eternity in our hearts enables us to have a concept of God and to understand what He has done for us. It is a foreshadowing of what lies ahead for us in eternity, when God removes the limitations from our hearts and minds.

Solomon's Concept of God

So how did Solomon view God? This will become clearer as we work through Ecclesiastes, but we have a few hints right here. More and more Solomon is bringing God to the forefront of his discussion.

Who is God? He didn't answer that question at this point. But he did point out a few characteristics of God as he understood Him.

He pictured God as an eternal being, able to do eternal things. What God set in motion would last forever. It was complete—humans can't add to it or take away from it. We see Solomon hinting at eternity here, but he didn't enlarge on what it meant to him. Was he expecting the universe to last forever? Or was he speaking of the souls of people, and the eternity in their hearts? He didn't say, but the context speaks of this, and he may well have been alluding to that.

He reiterated that God is actively involved in people's lives. People often are not satisfied with life the way God has patterned it and try to reason their way around His instructions and the limitations He has placed on them. This never works. It hasn't worked in the past, and it won't work in the future. As Solomon states, history tends to repeat itself, not blindly but under God's control.

Why does God do all of this? *So that people would fear Him.*

What kind of God did Solomon think he was serving? We'll get to that. But at this point his perspective of God was relatively generic.

FOR DISCUSSION

Read Ecclesiastes 3:9-15

Prelude

The prelude pictures Solomon taking a walk on a beautiful summer evening to relax after a trying day of work.

1. Read Psalm 8 and meditate on its message. Pondering the beauties of nature probably makes a good antidote for stress and despair, even for an unbeliever. But why would it be much more effective for someone who loves and follows God?

Work Is Travail

Some people find fulfillment in their work. Others just work for a paycheck and try to find fulfillment in their time off. Some people dream about retiring, and others dread the prospect.

2. In what ways does work add meaning to life? In what ways does it fail to do that?

3. How can you keep life from becoming a burden?

4. Is it wrong to look forward to retirement? How can you avoid having life lose its meaning if you don't have a job?

Everything Is Beautiful

We take life's simple joys and beauties for granted far too much of the time. Because of this we often miss some great blessings God has given us.

5. God created us with the ability to appreciate beauty. What does this tell us about God?

6. We can find beauty in nature, in music, and in literature. We can see it in the innocence of children, in the sound of a waterfall, and in the singing of birds. How does the ability to appreciate beauty—whether in nature, music, or literature—set us aside from the rest of God's creation?

7. How does beauty help us find meaning in life?

8. Why is it important to sometimes take time to "come apart and rest awhile"?

Eternity in Our Hearts

This concept is probably one that is overlooked by many people. In a sense, it is a divine attribute given to us by God—a foreshadowing of what is in store for us in eternity.

9. Without the gift of "eternity in our hearts," we would merely be "smart animals." Read Ecclesiastes 12:7 considering this. If we don't spend eternity with God, what will happen to the eternity in our hearts? What are the implications of this?

10. It seems likely that God placed limitations on the eternity in our hearts when Adam and Eve fell into sin and were denied access to the Tree of Life (See Genesis 3:22–24). Why would God deliberately limit our understanding and reasoning abilities?

Solomon's Concept of God

Solomon's concept of God seems to shift throughout the book of

Ecclesiastes. This could be because the process he described helped him to understand God better, or it could be because it fit his train of thought better.

11. Our concept of God tells us a lot about our relationship with Him. Why do you think this is true? What does this tell us about Solomon at this point in his life?

12. Are you trying to reason your way around God's direction? How can we tell if we are doing that?

Men Can Become Beasts

8

In the sweat of thy face shalt thou eat bread, till thou return unto the ground; for out of it wast thou taken: for dust thou art, and unto dust shalt thou return. Genesis 3:19

Prelude

Solomon wrote by inspiration, mostly. For the uninitiated, this means that sometimes he sat at his worktable doing nothing but staring out the window. Other times he puttered around his little workroom, straightening up things that weren't out of place and dusting spots that weren't dirty. But it also meant that sometimes he would sit hunched over his table writing as fast as he could with his reed pen.

At the moment, the whole palace was quiet and Solomon had thought of a good idea as he was preparing for bed. He lit a lamp, intending to quickly write down his thoughts before he forgot them. But now, several hours later, he was still sitting at his table, rereading what he had just written.

"So do men differ from animals when they die?" The question bothered him. According to the old writings, God had even told Adam, the firstborn of His creation, that he would go back to the dust when he died.

71

He knew that this was one question he would need to sort out before he fin-
ished his project, since it was at the root of his struggles. "Something is differ-
ent, though, I think. An animal couldn't take on a project like I am working
on. The sages and prophets who wrote the old writings believed that man has
something immortal within him. Something that allows God to touch him."

He watched the flame of his lamp flicker. It was almost out of oil, and he
would need to head back to bed before it left him in the dark. "I'm like that
lamp. My light will soon go out too. But will part of me keep on living?"

Still brooding over his thoughts, he picked up the lamp and walked into
his bedroom.

It is important to remember that Solomon approached his subject from a purely pragmatic perspective. Or, as mentioned before, he used observable data that anyone could see. He seemed to avoid evidence that required the reader to believe in supernatural or celestial perspectives. In this way, he seemed to be trying to bring agnostics and skeptics with him. This would explain verse 21 in this passage. He concluded the passage from this perspective—verse 22 is true even for an agnostic.

Note, however, his recognition that, in His own time, God would set all wrongs right.

When Beasts Try to Be Men

I once read a true story about a tame chimpanzee. He was young and had been "adopted" by a woman who treated him almost like a son. She taught him a rudimentary form of sign language. He sat at the table to eat, he smoked cigarettes, and he loved taking pictures with his camera.

People got quite excited about all this. In what way was this chimp different from a human being? The end of the account waxed quite eloquent about the link this provided between animals and humans.

But that wasn't the end of the real story. Several years later, I stumbled onto another magazine that picked up the story where the other one had left off. The chimp had started getting too big for his britches. (I believe he wore some clothing, so that might be more than just a cliché.) He became more and more uncontrollable until his owner was finally faced with the decision of how to get rid of him. Should she have him euthanized? Impossible—he was almost like her own flesh and blood. She didn't want him imprisoned in a zoo either. So finally she hired a woman experienced in jungle life to return him to his native habitat.

This was quite an experience for both the chimp and the woman responsible for getting him oriented to jungle life. Remember, the chimp had never seen the jungle, so he was horrified at his new environment. The first night they were in the jungle, he tried desperately to break into the safety of the woman's tent. Like any child spending the night in the jungle for the first time, he heard every sound and saw every shadow and it filled him with sheer terror.

His teacher had to start all over with his "education." She showed him how to scoop bugs off leaves for food. In fact, she ate them herself so he could imitate her and learn what was safe to eat. She spent months with him before she felt he had any chance of survival. Eventually, his long-stifled instincts started to kick in and helped him along. But it is hard to say how long he ended up surviving.

When animals try to imitate people, or when people act like animals, big trouble ensues.

When Men Act Like Beasts

In this passage, I think Solomon was

[16]And moreover I saw under the sun the place of judgment, that wickedness was there; and the place of righteousness, that iniquity was there. [17]I said in mine heart, God shall judge the righteous and the wicked: for there is a time there for every purpose and for every work. [18]I said in mine heart concerning the estate of the sons of men, that God might manifest them, and that they might see that they themselves are beasts. [19]For that which befalleth the sons of men befalleth beasts; even one thing befalleth them: as the one dieth, so dieth the other; yea, they have all one breath; so that a man hath no preeminence above a beast: for all is vanity. [20]All go unto one place; all are of the dust, and all turn to dust again. [21]Who knoweth the spirit of man that goeth upward, and the spirit of the beast that goeth downward to the earth? [22]Wherefore I perceive that there is nothing better, than that a man should rejoice in his own works; for that is his portion: for who shall bring him to see what shall be after him? (Eccles. 3:16-22)

pointing out that when men act like beasts they end up being no better than beasts. He gave two illustrations of men acting like beasts. He saw the judges in the place of justice mistreating innocent people. He also saw the religious leaders doing the same thing. The man who abuses his authority to take advantage of others is simply practicing the "survival of the fittest." In other words, he is acting like a beast rather than a man and is just as out of place in a human world as our chimpanzee friend was.

Solomon hinted that God sometimes allowed situations like this to show people what they really are. He also noted that God would eventually judge people who act like this.

When I think of men who act like beasts, I immediately think of two men who between them may have been responsible for more deaths than anyone else during the twentieth century. Hitler caused World War II. Fifty million people died because of World War II. About twelve million of these were innocent noncombatants who were killed directly by the German army.

Stalin comes next in line. Because of the lack of Soviet records from that time, it is hard to say how many people died under Stalin's administration. Estimates go as high as sixty million. Historians don't all agree, but most believe that the minimum estimate should be at least twenty million. Just to put that into perspective, it would be around 1,800 people per day for all thirty years that Stalin ruled the Soviet Union.

I didn't think of Mao Zedong, the Chinese leader, until I was researching the figures I gave in the last paragraphs.[1] Most historians consider Zedong to be responsible for more deaths than any other leader in modern history. At a minimum, forty-nine million people died because of him.[2] This is close to the number of people who died in World War II, which is considered the bloodiest war in history.

---

[1] He is better known as Mao Tse-tung, or Chairman Mao, by people in the West.

[2] I have read figures as high as seventy-eight million.

It's easy to see that men like these were acting like beasts.

But it can come closer to home than this. I've seen church leaders and fathers, and maybe an occasional mother and teacher, who ended up acting like dictators within their calling. Many of these are perhaps subconscious actions, but not all. I've heard people justify such actions from the Bible, and say that any father who doesn't rule his home with an iron hand isn't doing his God-given duty.

These ideas pass from generation to generation. Some personality types are also more susceptible to them. If such people get into a position of power, they default to becoming dictators. The difference between compassionate leadership and dictatorial leadership is almost like the difference between light and darkness. A good leader can have authority without stooping to the level of a dictator.

Your Heart Is Telling on You

Solomon included an idea in this passage that I've wondered about. Sometimes God puts us in situations which reveal what is in our heart. I have seen young men grow up very quickly once they became a father. The same thing can happen to a newly ordained church leader. I suspect that God sometimes chooses men to be fathers or church leaders because He wants to develop them further. Despite what many of us may think, God doesn't necessarily choose people for leadership because of their superior abilities or because they are extraordinarily yielded to God. Sometimes God wants to develop them further and place them in a position that reveals what is in their hearts. Leadership positions can do a lot of sorting out in people. It may be the most difficult test of all.

We have eternity in our heart. We have been given tremendous potential for enjoying life, as well as tremendous spiritual potential. Let's not be like the horse that plods through his day and sleeps through his night and never benefits from either. We need to find time to enjoy what God has given us today. And especially, we dare not let personal advantage trip us into acting like a beast. A beast doesn't understand justice, love, and kindness. We do. That makes us accountable for our actions.

Life lasts only for a lifetime, but it can be a tough road to walk. However, the person who follows God's direction can find simple joys in his or her calling. It is better to enjoy what God has given us now than to depend on dreams of a better future (see verse 22).

FOR DISCUSSION

Read Ecclesiastes 3:16-22

Prelude

A great divide exists between men and animals, even though many people today would like to deny that.

1. Think back over the last chapter. Why are people accountable to God, but animals aren't?

When Beasts Try to Be Men

Normally, beasts left to themselves don't try to "become" men.

2. Why do you think people like to "humanize" animals? What are the results from such efforts? Why?

When Men Act Like Beasts

"Humanizing" animals probably isn't so serious, but when men start to act like beasts (and even much worse), it becomes a different situation.

3. Sinful people, when given the opportunity, tend to become worse than animals. Why?

4. The Bible supports the concept of leadership authority in the church, as well as in the family. How can we keep this concept intact without deteriorating to dictatorship?

Your Heart Is Telling on You

God understands your heart better than you do.

5. What are some things God may bring into your life or allow to happen to show you what is in your heart?

6. How might you misunderstand this process? How can you benefit from it?

Life Under the Sun

*Fret not thyself because of evildoers, neither be thou envious against
the workers of iniquity. For they shall soon be cut down like the
grass, and wither as the green herb. Psalm 37:1, 2*

Prelude

*Solomon was sitting at his table and writing for a change rather than
watching the sunset. He was busy putting together a list of what he called
"Sure Things in Life." So far, his list had the following items:*

> *Death: Every person must die. Some live longer than others, but
> eventually everyone will die.*

> *Work: All humans must work, or they have no purpose for living.*

> *Evil: Every person will face evil and be tempted to do evil. Evil is a
> cancer that cannot be overcome.*

> *Oppression: The poor will be oppressed by those with more power and money.*

> *Judgment: Those who die, which is everyone, will be judged by God.*

*He stopped writing and looked critically at his list. "Why are all of life's
inevitable things negative?" He stroked his beard thoughtfully. "And does*

judgment really belong on it?"

He picked up his pen as if to stroke the last entry off his list. But then he hesitated and laid it down again. "Judgment isn't part of this life," he mused, "but a lot of bad things will be set straight in judgment. So it does influence life."

His window was open, and as he pondered, he watched the evening star appear over the horizon. Slowly he picked up his pen again and continued writing.

In a sense, Solomon is reflecting on the realities of life in this chapter. Here you see the Solomon who wrote Proverbs surfacing for a few moments. In one way these thoughts are just that—thoughts. Maybe even musings. Yet they do address issues that we face as we try to sort out life. Power, oppression, security, success—we run into all of them as we go through life. And we leave all of them behind when we leave this life.

The Reality of Oppression (4:1–7)

Solomon examined oppression from a philosophical perspective in this passage rather than from a sympathetic or philanthropic one. In fact, oppression was one of the accusations that the northern tribes later leveled against him when they rebelled against his son Rehoboam. Solomon was a king, which in those days meant he was a dictator. Had he been concerned about oppression or believed it was wrong, he could have done something about it.

It seems more likely that he was merely stating the fact that oppression is one of the realities of life. I know that some people like to use this passage and the one in 5:8 to promote the idea of human rights. I am not against protecting people from oppression and misuse, but I don't think this is what Solomon was talking about. I think he was simply defining various realities of life. He strayed from that perspective at times, but ended up returning to it sooner or later. After all, many of the realities of life for most people throughout history have been negative.

Solomon clearly recognized this, and that is part of the reason for the depressing atmosphere of Ecclesiastes. Many of those reading this book (I assume) have been sheltered from some of these negative realities of life. But that is not the historical norm, even for God's people. And even today, it isn't the norm for most of the earth's population. We can shrug that off, but we should not emulate Solomon's approach to this subject by simply looking at it from an academic perspective and leaving it at that.

In the parable of the Good Samaritan, the priest and the Levite took that perspective. The priest pretended not to see the injured man, but the Levite added insult to injury by walking over to the victim and looking him over before continuing his way. Talk about being hard-hearted! He was probably curious if he knew the man, and when he didn't, he didn't worry about him anymore.

I wonder if his conscience bothered him that night.

Solomon described the case of the oppressed clearly. The oppressors were powerful, which insinuates that the oppressed had no hope of justice. The oppressed cried and had no one to comfort them. In fact, Solomon noted that death was a favor to the oppressed and the only relief they could expect. But it would have been even better, he added, if they had never been born.

I am sure many people in the world today, and in history, have

> [1]So I returned, and considered all the oppressions that are done under the sun: and behold the tears of such as were oppressed, and they had no comforter; and on the side of their oppressors there was power; but they had no comforter. [2]Wherefore I praised the dead which are already dead more than the living which are yet alive. [3]Yea, better is he than both they, which hath not yet been, who hath not seen the evil work that is done under the sun. [4]Again, I considered all travail, and every right work, that for this a man is envied of his neighbour. This is also vanity and vexation of spirit. [5]The fool foldeth his hands together, and eateth his own flesh. [6]Better is an handful with quietness, than both the hands full with travail and vexation of spirit. [7]Then I returned, and I saw vanity under the sun. (Eccles. 4:1-7)

wished they had never been born. We can't help them all, but Christian love should constrain us to help those we can. Sometimes Christians are afraid of what we call a social gospel, focusing more on physical needs than on spiritual ones. Missions have even closed medical clinics for that reason. But the Bible tells us clearly how God views that kind of approach:

> If a brother or sister be naked, and destitute of daily food, And one of you say unto them, Depart in peace, be ye warmed and filled; notwithstanding ye give them not those things which are needful to the body; what doth it profit? (James 2:15, 16)

Solomon was a child of his time. I don't think he was cold and hardhearted as far as the needs of others went. But in the time and era he lived in, the king was absolute authority. He didn't have a problem with that, and this passage probably reflects that. Bear in mind also that he was giving us snapshots, and he didn't muddy the waters in these pictures by bringing in a lot of subjects or ideas that would sidetrack the discussion.

Security in Numbers (4:8-12)

The idea of community no longer seems to be in vogue today. People revel in their independence and avoid depending on others if possible. Even farming is different. Gone are the days of the old threshing rings. Most farmers own their own equipment, or they may hire a custom operator to do some work, if necessary.

Solomon used the illustration of an

8There is one alone, and there is not a second; yea, he hath neither child nor brother: yet is there no end of all his labour; neither is his eye satisfied with riches; neither saith he, For whom do I labour, and bereave my soul of good? This is also vanity, yea, it is a sore travail. 9Two are better than one; because they have a good reward for their labour. 10For if they fall, the one will lift up his fellow: but woe to him that is alone when he falleth; for he hath not another to help him up. 11Again, if two lie together, then they have heat: but how can one be warm alone? 12And if one prevail against him, two shall withstand him; and a threefold cord is not quickly broken. (Eccles. 4:8-12)

Searching for Meaning

independent person to show what he was talking about. Normally people work for more than the "joy" of working. They may have a family to support, or some other reason. But here was a man who, apparently, had no reason to work except to accumulate money. He had no heirs—no children or other family members—to give his wealth to when he died. He didn't even take time off to enjoy himself. His only reason for getting up in the morning was doing more work and making more money.

Independence and a big bank account will never help us find meaning in life. Solomon gave various illustrations to show that two or three people together are better off than one person by himself. This is another reality of life.

You were not created to be a loner. God made you a social being, and you will never find fulfillment in life without friends or family.

Success Is Short-Lived (4:13-16)

Strange things happen. Joseph was sold as a slave and ended up ruling Egypt, the most powerful nation at that time. Daniel became the chief of the three presidents of the Medes and Persians. But this isn't the norm, and if we expect miraculous promotions like this to help us find meaning in life, we will probably be disappointed.

This kind of incident seldom outlasts the person who experiences them. In Daniel's case, the princes and presidents of the Medes and Persians coerced King Darius to throw Daniel into a lions' den. Daniel survived this, but life in the king's court was dicey at best.

> [13]Better is a poor and a wise child than an old and foolish king, who will no more be admonished. [14]For out of prison he cometh to reign; whereas also he that is born in his kingdom becometh poor. [15]I considered all the living which walk under the sun, with the second child that shall stand up in his stead. [16]There is no end of all the people, even of all that have been before them: they also that come after shall not rejoice in him. Surely this also is vanity and vexation of spirit. (Eccles. 4:13-16)

You and I will be mostly forgotten within a few years after we die. And in some cases, we might be forgotten by most people even before we die.

That is another reality of life.

FOR DISCUSSION

Read Ecclesiastes 4:1-16

Prelude

In the prelude Solomon asks the question, "Why are all of life's inevitable things negative?"

1. Is this true? Or was Solomon simply feeling negatively about life?

2. What are some positive things about life that are inevitable as well?

The Reality of Oppression

Many people blame God for allowing oppression and wonder why He doesn't stop it. But Solomon seems to take oppression for granted as if it were a normal part of living.

3. Do you think God views oppression like Solomon seemed to view it? Why or why not?

4. Many of God's children have been oppressed throughout history. This doesn't seem fair to us as Christians. Considering 1 Peter 4:12-19, how do you think God views this?

5. Possibly the worst kind of oppression is the kind instigated or supported by people who profess to be Christians. How should we react to this? Read James 2:1-13.

Security in Numbers

People love their independence today. In many cities people don't even know who their neighbors are.

6. How does today's spirit of independence help to destroy society? How does the lack of community spirit destroy meaning in life?

7. God has set up a community for His children called the church. He intends these communities of believers to give spiritual security and joy to Christians. Read Revelation 3:1–13. Which of these two churches would you want to be part of? Why? Which of the two more closely resembles your church?

8. In what way would it be better to be part of the church at Sardis than to not be part of a church at all?

Success Is Short-Lived

9. Do you think becoming a well-known singer, actor, or politician would help you find meaning in life? Explain your answer.

10. Why do you think the idea of being forgotten might have bothered Solomon?

God Hears What You Say

10

Who is this that darkeneth counsel by words without knowledge?
Gird up now thy loins like a man; for I will demand of thee, and
answer thou me. Job 38:2, 3

Prelude

Solomon woke up early, thinking about an old scroll in his collection. So the
first thing he did that morning was go into his thinking room and look for it.
It took him a bit of time because he wasn't quite sure what he was looking for.
When he did find it, he discovered that it was several scrolls—three, in fact.

He laid them carefully on his worktable and just as carefully started to look
through them. They were even older than he had thought and had no signa-
ture or title. They were written in an ancient form of Hebrew, or a language
like Hebrew. An old scholar from Edom had given them to him, with the sug-
gestion that they gave the account of an ancient follower of the true God—one
who had lived before the kingdom of Israel even existed.

"It's been years since I read these scrolls," Solomon mused. "But if I remem-
ber correctly, the author was struggling with some of the same questions about
God that I have."

He continued to scan through the first scroll but didn't find what he was looking for, so he picked up the last one. He remembered now that he had numbered them so he could see the sequence of the content.

"I think it was toward the end," he muttered to himself. "God actually spoke to him and challenged him to show how much knowledge he had by asking him questions. I remember how intrigued I was by the account. Strange that I haven't thought of this for so long."

He paused in his reading. "Here it is. This is what I was looking for." He smoothed out the old scroll carefully and started to read.

"Then the LORD answered Job out of the whirlwind and said . . ."[1]

―――――――――――――

For the first time in Ecclesiastes, we see Solomon painting a portrait that seems to show a real respect for God. He had mentioned God earlier, but not really in a personal way. This probably tells us more about Solomon than it does about God.

I am uneasy about delving too deeply into analyzing God or predicting what God would think or say about certain situations. As humans, we don't really know that much about God. I wonder how often God feels like telling us what He told Job, that we are "darkening counsel by words without knowledge."

Solomon's passages about God are in the Bible for a reason, however. I think it is good for us to look at them and learn from them what we can. Solomon delved into this subject with three warnings for us.

Watch Your Step

Solomon seemed to be speaking about going to the temple in this passage, though this passage has applications that go far beyond that. He started

―――――――――――――

[1] The book of Job appears to relate an ancient account which may have taken place between Babel and the time of Abraham. Job was not a Jew and probably represented an alternate trail of faith in God. The Bible hints several times that the knowledge of God was spread far and wide during the early centuries after the flood. It could easily be that in some of these countries undocumented believers had kept the knowledge of God alive on a family level by handing down oral or written traditions about Him. Somehow Job's account became attached to the Old Testament Scriptures and was handed down with them. I think it is entirely possible that Solomon had managed to put together a collection of such items. He would certainly have been interested in the account of Job, if he had access to it.

out by warning us to be careful when we go to meet God. Some translations begin verse one with "guard your steps." In other words, watch your actions and don't be rude and arrogant. God is in heaven, and you are only here on earth, so don't make a fool out of yourself.

We'll come back to this subject when we look at chapter 8, but I get the impression that Solomon is saying to himself, "I know how God feels when these foolish people come into His presence with brash demands." Solomon was a king and had lots of experience with people who acted like that. He was warning us to be respectful when we meet God and speak to Him.

When I was teaching school I unlocked the door one morning after some students had already arrived. It was the first day the kindergarten class was coming to school.

> [1]Keep thy foot when thou goest to the house of God, and be more ready to hear, than to give the sacrifice of fools: for they consider not that they do evil. [2]Be not rash with thy mouth, and let not thine heart be hasty to utter any thing before God: for God is in heaven, and thou upon earth: therefore let thy words be few. [3]For a dream cometh through the multitude of business; and a fool's voice is known by multitude of words. [4]When thou vowest a vow unto God, defer not to pay it; for he hath no pleasure in fools: pay that which thou hast vowed. [5]Better is it that thou shouldest not vow, than that thou shouldest vow and not pay. [6]Suffer not thy mouth to cause thy flesh to sin; neither say thou before the angel, that it was an error: wherefore should God be angry at thy voice, and destroy the work of thine hands? [7]For in the multitude of dreams and many words there are also divers vanities: but fear thou God. (Eccles. 5:1-7)

One youngster walked up to me and asked—about as insolently as it sounds—if I didn't work. Ouch! I suspect he was only repeating something he had heard elsewhere, as in that circle some people tended to view male teachers as lazy and afraid to get their hands dirty. I must admit that it irritated me, and I've never forgotten it. I'm grateful that God is more willing to forget such things about me than I am sometimes able to forget them about others.

However, God does note attitudes and He has His ways of humbling us when we get too conceited. We must never go to church to tell God or His people where they have it all wrong. Instead, we should go to listen and to learn.

Don't Talk Too Much

Recently I overheard someone comment about people who "fill the air with words." You can probably think of someone right now who fits that description. We all know people who talk too much. Sometimes *we* talk too much as well.

Solomon made some interesting statements in this passage about talking too much. First, we can be rash or hasty in talking. As Solomon said, God is in heaven and we are on earth, so we would do better to let our words be few. It says here that a fool's voice is known by a multitude of words. In Proverbs 10:19, Solomon said that "in the multitude of words there wanteth not sin." Too often we hear people babble on about things, only to turn around and deny that they said what people understood them to say.

All writers, public speakers, and teachers need to learn to be concise, precise, and deliberate with their words, rather than simply "filling the air with words."

Keep Your Promises

It is easy to make promises on the spur of the moment. But it is harder to keep those promises when the moment has come and gone. I remember reading several versions of the account of a man who fell off a cliff but managed to grab a little tree growing from the side of the cliff. As he hung there, he begged and pleaded with God to save him, promising to serve him for the rest of his life if he did. God answered him, saying, "I think I have heard you make promises like that before."

The man replied, "I'm *serious* this time. I'll do anything you want me to do."

To which God replied, "Okay, let go of the tree."

People have added various endings to this little story, but I don't think we need an ending to get the point. According to one version of the story, the man died there, still somehow hanging on to the tree. The people who found him discovered that he was hanging about a foot above a ledge and would have been perfectly safe in letting go. But the point of the original story was that we shouldn't be too quick to make rash promises that we won't keep, and maybe even can't keep.

Promises are especially serious when we make them to God. This could include promises like marriage vows and baptismal vows. Solomon stated that it would be better not to make a promise than to not keep it. He gave an illustration of this in verse 6. The word "angel" here simply means messenger in Hebrew. It appears that a man had made a pledge that he would pay a certain amount against a need or a project. But when an agent came to claim his pledge, he couldn't pay it or had a change of heart and tried to tell him that it was a misunderstanding. God doesn't take kindly to such excuses.

Solomon was thinking of words and promises we make to God. But I think the principle holds in other situations too. We can build up a reputation for foolish talking by telling stretched stories and stupid jokes, or even by just talking all the time. Or we can even get a reputation for dishonesty by promising to pay bills or loans by a certain time and not getting it done.

In Summary
Go back and reread Ecclesiastes 5:1-7. Put yourself in Solomon's sandals and try to read his mind as you read this passage. What kind of picture is he painting of God? These verses contain a lot of good thoughts about speaking, but I'm just as interested in what they show us about Solomon's perspective of God.

I wish the Bible would give us a more detailed time line of Solomon's life. But given the details he gave in the first chapters, he must have written this book toward the end of his life. So this is the best indication we have about his frame of mind at the end of life.

I'm going to suggest a few things here and then come back to this when we look at chapter 8.

First, he viewed God as a real being. He pictures God as being able to hear what we say and take seriously what we promise Him. He also sees God as having likes and dislikes—He doesn't like fools, for instance. God has feelings as well; He can be offended and get angry. He may even lash out at you and destroy the work of your hands if you displease him. He repeats that warning several times throughout Ecclesiastes.

It seems that Solomon viewed God as sort of a mirror image of himself with supernatural powers.

FOR DISCUSSION

Read Ecclesiastes 5:1-7

Prelude

Job and Solomon both asked "why." Job couldn't understand why God allowed bad things to happen to good people. Solomon couldn't understand why life didn't make more sense if God was in control.

1. Read Romans 11:33-36. What did both Job and Solomon need to learn about God?

Watch Your Step

People say foolish things about God, or even to God, sometimes. Solomon apparently had seen some of this.

2. Read Isaiah 2:11-17 and discuss God's reaction to our pride.

3. Contrast this with Ephesians 2:4-7. This is the side of God that Solomon didn't seem to know as much about.

Don't Talk Too Much

When people talk too much, their words tend to mean less.

4. How would Matthew 12:36, 37 fit into this section? What are idle words? How might our words justify us or condemn us?

Keep Your Promises

A promise not kept turns into a lie. We should take our words seriously.

5. It could be that Solomon was thinking of Deuteronomy 23:21-23 when he wrote Ecclesiastes 5:4, 5. Compare these two passages. What practical applications can you think of for these passages?

6. What about promises we make to people?

In Summary

The author suggests that Solomon viewed God as being "a mirror image of himself with supernatural powers."

7. Do you agree with this? Why or why not?

Riches Never Satisfy

Lay not up for yourselves treasures upon earth, where moth and rust doth corrupt, and where thieves break through and steal: But lay up for yourselves treasures in heaven, where neither moth nor rust doth corrupt, and where thieves do not break through nor steal: Matthew 6:19, 20

Prelude

Solomon had given the daily operations of his household over to his steward, who had been his loyal servant for many years. In fact, Solomon trusted him so far that he seldom paid any attention to what he was doing or asked him to account for the money he spent. But just today he had learned that the steward had been cheating him for years and using royal money to finance a gambling addiction.

As usual, when faced with a crisis, Solomon was in his thinking room.

"I wonder how much of my money he has taken over the years." Solomon clenched his fists. "I thought he was a friend of mine. I should have him whipped in the marketplace for taking advantage of me like that. Did he really think he would never be caught?"

He spun on his heel as the chief officer of his guard entered the room. "What have you found out?" Solomon asked. "Have you questioned him?"

"He hanged himself in his cell, using his girdle strap," the officer said matter-of-factly. "We found him there about five minutes ago. He was already cold, so he must have done it soon after we locked him up."

It took Solomon a moment to digest this unexpected information. "So he couldn't handle facing justice." Solomon's question was really a statement, but the officer nodded his head.

Solomon looked out the window before continuing. "Give the body to his family," he said finally. "And make sure they have the help they need to look after it."

The officer hesitated a moment. "Shall we continue to investigate whether we can retrieve any of the money?"

Solomon shook his head. "It will only make a greater hardship for his family if they have to pay his debt. I'm sure he spent it all, and they never saw much benefit from it."

The officer nodded again and turned to leave as Solomon added, "Assure them that they will not be held accountable for his sins."

The love of money has done much damage to many people. In this section, Solomon returned to this idea in greater detail. He liked money and possessions well enough himself, but he had learned the hard way that it didn't bring happiness. This reality is a difficult one for many people to learn and deal with.

The New Testament states it this way: "But they that will be rich fall into temptation and a snare, and into many foolish and hurtful lusts, which drown men in destruction and perdition. For the love of money is the root of all evil" (1 Tim. 6:9–10). Solomon would have agreed with this, had he seen it.

Here are a few ways that the love of money affects people.

Corruption (5:8, 9)

Solomon, again, looked at his subject from a philosophical perspective, not a human rights perspective. The poor were oppressed by those who were stronger than they were or who had more authority. Those people in turn were oppressed by those above them. The chain of oppression reached all the way to the top, and may have even included the king.[1] Perversion of justice is very common. In some countries, a person is better off accepting oppression than reporting it or trying to get justice. Solomon wasn't commenting on the right or wrong of this (it is obviously wrong). Instead, he was describing a basic reality of life along with a little lesson on economics.

Solomon used a field as a simple example of economic supply and demand. Many people needed to live from the economic product of the field. The people who planted the field, watered it, and harvested it were the most obvious economic beneficiaries. In Bible times these people didn't own the field or finance the crop, they were just laborers who were paid for their work. Of course, the man who owned the field also needed to receive a benefit. He may have sold the crop to a miller, who produced flour from it. That man also needed to make some income from the field's product to feed his family, so he sold the flour to a baker, who baked bread and sold it to a local store. The local store finally sold it to the person who ate it.[2] So the laborers, the farmer, the miller, the baker, and the store all needed to have a share of the economic product of the field.

> [8]If thou seest the oppression of the poor, and violent perverting of judgment and justice in a province, marvel not at the matter: for he that is higher than the highest regardeth; and there be higher than they. [9]Moreover the profit of the earth is for all: the king himself is served by the field. (Eccles. 5:8, 9)

---

[1] This is another passage that requires some thought and could be taken various ways. If you compare various translations, you will understand why I took the course I did here. I would especially recommend the translation notes in the New English Translation (NET).

[2] Not every step is necessarily present all the time. The householder in Bible times probably bought the flour and baked his own bread. The poorer people probably bought grain and ground it and baked their own bread. The baker probably took the bread to a local market and sold it directly to the householder, but he probably had to pay a fee to the market owner. These principles take many different shapes, but the basic principle Solomon gave here is part of the economic cycle everywhere.

But the process goes beyond that. Some of these people might have borrowed money to finance their operations, so the economic product of the field also paid the interest on their loans. And finally, the government collected taxes from these people. So even the government lived from the field's economic product.

Now none of this is wrong. But it does give a lot of opportunity for *doing* wrong. At any link of this economic chain, someone could oppress the person who depended on him for his income. The most vulnerable ones, of course, are those at the bottom of the ladder. If the farmer was greedy and many people were looking for work in the fields, he could make extra money by paying unfair wages. The laborers had little recourse because they had less money and less authority and fewer powerful friends than the farmer did.

Some people try to take advantage of others by bribing them. Some threaten them by using their authority. And on and on it goes. The king (i.e., the government) was at the top of the ladder and had the most power and authority of all. It is easy for government to use this power to take advantage of the population.

The process of corruption is prompted by greed, of course. But it is also prompted by the fact that the economic resources of the field are limited. You can stretch a natural resource only so far. The people in line for getting a piece of the pie are afraid that the economic profit won't reach around, so they fight over it. In cases like this it isn't the early bird that gets the worm. Rather, the biggest bird gets it, even though he may be the last one to reach the table.

People living in democratic countries like to think that these things happen only in third-world countries or countries run by dictators. But anyone studying the effects of capitalism, lobbying, and big money in our time will soon realize that these things happen to us as well.

Corruption is one of the realities caused by the love of money. If we depend on money for happiness or meaning in life, we will be disappointed—which, I believe, was Solomon's point in these verses.

Covetousness (5:10-12)

These verses contain several interesting statements about money. First, *if your satisfaction in life is based on money, you will never have enough money to satisfy you.* You will never be satisfied with your income. You will always want more.

10He that loveth silver shall not be satisfied with silver; nor he that loveth abundance with increase: this is also vanity. 11When goods increase, they are increased that eat them: and what good is there to the owners thereof, saving the beholding of them with their eyes? 12The sleep of a labouring man is sweet, whether he eat little or much: but the abundance of the rich will not suffer him to sleep. (Eccles. 5:10-12)

The second observation is one that you probably won't find in a textbook on principles of economics, either. *The more money you have or the higher your income, the more it will cost you to live.* You will have more needs and more people to feed and more places you need to go. Unless you deliberately start a savings plan and stick to it no matter what, you won't get much money saved. Most people can identify with that.

So what is the advantage of having a better income? According to this passage, there is only one advantage—you will get to see more money as it slips through your fingers. Or to put it in business terms, you will have a higher cash flow. But at the end of the week or the end of the year, you won't have any more left than you did before.

That sounds a bit cynical. In fact, my first impression of this whole section was that Solomon had slipped back into his cynicism. But I think he was trying to be honest about the realities of life and the problems that accompany money—*especially if that is what you live for.*

The last principle here is a bit of a twist in logic. *If you work hard, you will sleep well.* Even if you don't have much money. Even if you go to bed hungry. That seems like a paradox, given that people who need to go to bed hungry often have financial worries to keep them awake. But I guess if you are working hard enough, you will sleep anyway.

Solomon was making a point—wealth doesn't help you sleep. Instead, it hinders you from sleeping. Since it doesn't bring satisfaction and since you can never get enough, you will lie awake at night trying to figure out how to invest your money to make more money. Or you will worry about someone stealing it. Or you may worry about someone taking you or your family hostage and demanding a large ransom. A wealthy person has no end of worries to keep him awake, as Solomon knew very well.

Riches Are Fleeting (5:13-17)

I once knew a man who saw an opportunity to pay off his farm by selling his crop on the future's market.[3] This means that he sold it at an exceptionally good price, months before it was ready to harvest. Unfortunately for him, a hailstorm destroyed his crop. However, his contract stated that he still needed to supply the grain he had presold. So he had to buy enough grain on the open market to meet his obligations. But the storm had destroyed other people's crops as well. This made a shortage of that kind of grain and the price on the open market was quite a bit higher than the price he had contracted for. So he lost nearly as much money as he had expected to make. Instead of paying his farm off in one grand swoop, he almost lost it.

> [13]There is a sore evil which I have seen under the sun, namely, riches kept for the owners thereof to their hurt. [14]But those riches perish by evil travail: and he begetteth a son, and there is nothing in his hand. [15]As he came forth of his mother's womb, naked shall he return to go as he came, and shall take nothing of his labour, which he may carry away in his hand. [16]And this also is a sore evil, that in all points as he came, so shall he go: and what profit hath he that hath laboured for the wind? [17]All his days also he eateth in darkness, and he hath much sorrow and wrath with his sickness. (Eccles. 5:13-17)

In Proverbs 23:5 Solomon wrote that "riches certainly make themselves wings; they fly away as an eagle toward heaven." Here in Ecclesiastes we find a similar idea. The man in this passage had hoarded his money, expecting to use it to make more money. However, because of a bad business decision or some other misfortune, he lost it all. Apparently he was

---

[3] An unwise thing to do, though some farmers have made a lot of money by doing so.

Searching for Meaning

never able to replace it, though he worked from dawn until dusk. He ate his breakfast in the dark and didn't come in for supper until it was dark again. But it was all to no avail. His son, instead of being heir to a large inheritance, got nothing.

When he died, he owned no more than when he was born. He was a sick and angry man, a total failure—at least from the world's perspective, which is the way Solomon was looking at it here.

Enjoy the Fruit of Your Labor (5:18-20)

Solomon really laid it on in this chapter. He seemed determined to prove the futility of seeking meaning or satisfaction in life by accumulating riches. As the richest man of his generation, he probably knew what he was talking about. Though I have to wonder, if riches were such a problem, why didn't he just give his away? He could have lived comfortably on a tenth of his net worth. But maybe he was like most of us and found it easier to give good advice than to take it. If you read Proverbs and compare it with his actual life, you can't help but wonder if that wasn't part of his problem.

Suddenly, however, Solomon switches gears and points out that not everything about money is negative. What he says here seems to contradict his earlier sentiments, and we find ourselves wondering how to reconcile the two. I believe Solomon had the same problem. But like a lawyer in a courtroom, he is examining the evidence, both the good and the bad.

He tells us that it is good for a man to enjoy the good he gets from his work—the blessings of having enough to eat and to drink. He advises us to take satisfaction in a job well done and to accept our lot in life and be content. According to verse 12 we

> [18]Behold that which I have seen: it is good and comely for one to eat and to drink, and to enjoy the good of all his labour that he taketh under the sun all the days of his life, which God giveth him: for it is his portion. [19]Every man also to whom God hath given riches and wealth, and hath given him power to eat thereof, and to take his portion, and to rejoice in his labour; this is the gift of God. [20]For he shall not much remember the days of his life; because God answereth him in the joy of his heart. (Eccles. 5:18-20)

should even be able to sleep well!

Was Solomon being a bit sarcastic in this passage? I'm not sure, but his tone strikes me as tongue-in-cheek, because immediately after these positive statements we see another twist in his logic.

God does this, he says, to keep you from brooding over the past, as several translations put it. He wants to keep you occupied and out of trouble, so He lets you be happy. Solomon left out the bottom line, but I think it's there—he just doesn't say it: Any happiness caused by accumulating money and possessions is just an illusion, a mirage in the desert that keeps moving away from you, mocking you by promising you relief that doesn't even exist.

The Futility of Craving for More (6:1-9)

Here it is—the other side of the story. This passage gives us the account of a man who seemed to have it made. He had wealth and honor, and everything else that his heart could desire. But he never got to enjoy it because he died an untimely death. Perhaps he became ill or maybe he had an accident with his chariot. Anyway, he never lived to enjoy what he had accumulated.

He may have had all kinds of plans for retirement. Or maybe he was going to double his riches in the next ten years through wise investments. But it was all an illusion—another mirage that didn't exist.

> ¹There is an evil which I have seen under the sun, and it is common among men: ²A man to whom God hath given riches, wealth, and honour, so that he wanteth nothing for his soul of all that he desireth, yet God giveth him not power to eat thereof, but a stranger eateth it: this is vanity, and it is an evil disease. ³If a man beget an hundred children, and live many years, so that the days of his years be many, and his soul be not filled with good, and also that he have no burial; I say, that an untimely birth is better than he. ⁴For he cometh in with vanity, and departeth in darkness, and his name shall be covered with darkness. ⁵Moreover he hath not seen the sun, nor known any thing: this hath more rest than the other. ⁶Yea, though he live a thousand years twice told, yet hath he seen no good: do not all go to one place? ⁷All the labour of man is for his mouth, and yet the appetite is not filled. ⁸For what hath the wise more than the fool? what hath the poor, that knoweth to walk before the living? ⁹Better is the sight of the eyes than the wandering of the desire: this is also vanity and vexation of spirit. (Eccles. 6:1-9)

Really, that is all riches can give you—an illusion of happiness. It can never bring true happiness or meaning in life.

Solomon went on to list other things that gave a similar illusion. For instance, would having a hundred children help you find meaning in life? The understood answer is no. If you haven't found it some other way, it would be better for you if you had never been born, or been stillborn.

Even if you managed to live for several thousand years, nothing would change if you hadn't found contentment somehow. After all, you will still need to die sometime. And when you finally do die, you will die just like everyone else.

So really, he finally concluded, you are much better off enjoying the little you have and being content. That is a lot better than dreaming about having great riches or being an important person. Or, in today's terms, it is better than owning a large business empire or a fancy mansion or becoming the president of the United States.

Don't crave what God hasn't given you. Be content with what you have. In New Testament terms, find your contentment in being a child of God and what He has done for you.

Only God Knows the Future (6:10-12)

You have no power to decide your future, according to Solomon. It may be that Solomon believed at this point that God was just the equivalent of fate and that our destiny was fixed before we were ever born. That conclusion doesn't jibe with his later conclusions, nor does it find any support in the New Testament. But as Solomon looked at life, that's what it seemed like to him.

[10]That which hath been is named already, and it is known that it is man: neither may he contend with him that is mightier than he. [11]Seeing there be many things that increase vanity, what is man the better? [12]For who knoweth what is good for man in this life, all the days of his vain life which he spendeth as a shadow? for who can tell a man what shall be after him under the sun? (Eccles. 6:10-12)

FOR DISCUSSION

Read Ecclesiastes 5:8–6:12

Prelude

The love of money has destroyed many people. But money never brings meaning to life. Solomon learned this the hard way.

1. The Bible doesn't say that *money* is sinful, but rather that the *love of money* is the problem. Why do you think it makes this distinction?

Corruption

The study of economic processes is interesting, but the processes themselves are not wrong. However, they lead to a great deal of wrongdoing.

2. How do corruption and greed work together? How do they keep people from finding happiness or meaning in life by accumulating money?

Covetousness

I enjoy Solomon's down-to-earth observations about money. We can certainly see a lot of truth in these verses.

3. What are the two economic principles pointed out here? What can we learn from them?

4. How does the love of money strengthen these principles?

5. Solomon probably didn't write Proverbs 30:8, 9. Discuss the implications that this passage adds to what he wrote in Ecclesiastes.

Riches Are Fleeting

I have seen pictures of dollar bills with wings. Proverbs 23:4, 5 gives us a similar picture.

6. North America is a rich continent. In what ways might riches be fleeting even in North America?

Searching for Meaning

Enjoy the Fruit of Your Labor

The book of Ecclesiastes contains lots of statements that seem contradictory. In most cases both statements are needed to get the complete picture. In other cases, Solomon seems to use them to add color.

7. In what ways is the idea of gaining happiness by accumulating money and possessions just a mirage?

8. How is finding satisfaction in a job well done and enjoying the fruit of our labor different from finding meaning in life from our work and possessions?

The Futility of Craving for More

Aesop wrote in his fables that *much wants more and loses all.* In a nutshell, that summarizes Ecclesiastes 6:1-9.

9. Some people crave expensive vehicles. Others like fancy houses or clothing. How can a lack of contentment become a trap for you? What is the secret of finding contentment? (See Hebrews 13:5.)

Only God Knows the Future

The idea of fate would have fit well with the cynicism Solomon expressed earlier in this book. In fact, the idea that we and everything around us are preprogrammed and without choice or free will would have pleased Solomon because it would have vindicated his doubts about God.

10. Find some New Testament passages that teach the free will of man. (Read 1 Timothy 2:3-6 for a starter.)

The Contrast of Wisdom and Folly

12

If a wise man contendeth with a foolish man,
whether he rage or laugh, there is no rest. Proverbs 29:9

Prelude

Solomon had written a lot about wisdom when he was younger. But now,
looking back, he wondered if things were really as simple as he had thought
they were. He considered himself to be wise, and God had promised him
special wisdom. Yet as he sat pondering his years of ruling God's people, he
wondered if some of his decisions were as wise as he had thought they were.

He moved over to the window in his thinking room and watched the sun
setting in the west. He loved sunrises and sunsets, but he couldn't watch
the sunrise without going outside, so he found himself watching the sunset
more often. Usually it helped to brighten his perspective, but not tonight.
He could feel the gloom descending on him as darkness fell outside.

"People say I'm the wisest man in the world," he thought. "So why have
I made so many foolish choices?"

He thought of his son Rehoboam. "I've let him go his own way, just like my father did with Absalom. Now he seems to think he will do a much better job of ruling Israel than I have. But I can't tell him anything. He'll have to learn for himself."

He settled into his chair and leaned his elbows on his writing table. "And Rehoboam isn't the only one who feels that way about me. I've gotten a lot accomplished, but the cost in human labor has been enormous. A lot of people would be glad to see Rehoboam take my place. They seem to think he wouldn't be such a hard taskmaster."

He remembered how the Israelites had thronged his father at public events. "Everyone loved him. But I wonder if anyone still loves me."

Had his life been dominated by wisdom, or folly? Maybe that would make a good subject for his ongoing project. One thing was sure—folly didn't help bring meaning to life.

Good choices are always better than bad ones. But we need wisdom to make truly good choices, not just some we could term as merely acceptable. Solomon gave some examples of each of these in the first ten verses of this chapter.

Contrasts Illustrating Wisdom (7:1-10)

This passage contains various proverbs, most of which introduce a contrast. The following chart summarizes these. Not all the choices listed in the "inferior" column are wrong or bad, but all of them are inferior to the choices in the third column.

You can read down through this list yourself and learn from it. But I am especially interested in what it tells us about Solomon's personality.

What kind of person do you think Solomon was? Look at his statements. The day of your death is better than the day of your birth. It is better to go to a funeral than to a party. It is better to sorrow than to laugh. In fact, he denigrates laughter three or four times. Was Solomon an "old fogey" who simply didn't enjoy fun? Was he getting

Verse	Inferior	Wise
7:1	precious ointment (perfume)	a good reputation
7:1	day of your birth	day of your death
7:2	going to a feast	going to a funeral
7:3	laughing	sorrowing
7:4	the house of mirth	the house of mourning
7:5	praise from a fool	the rebuke of a wise person
7:6	the laughter of the fool	seriousness (assumed)
7:7	oppression	kindness (assumed)
7:7	bribery	honesty (assumed)
7:8	the beginning of something	the end of the same thing
7:8	pride	patience
7:9	anger	not easily provoked
7:10	the old days	today

too old? I don't think so. In fact, Solomon said elsewhere that "a merry heart doeth good like a medicine" (Prov. 17:22). But when you look down the "inferior" column, you start to visualize a certain kind of person—someone who could get excited about something new but had a hard time sticking it out. Someone who enjoyed taking the easy route through life. Someone who would rather tell a joke than quote a Bible verse. Someone who wanted his own pleasure, even if it came at someone else's cost or hurt.

The third column doesn't list the easy way out. All these options are harder and less exciting than the alternative. But in the end, these wise choices help a person grow and be useful—to become the kind of person you go to when you need some down-to-earth good advice.[1]

Verse 10 seems rather odd when you contrast it with the first nine verses. Many of the people who fit the descriptions in the "wise"

---

[1] I find it hard to reconcile the Solomon I see in passages like this with the Solomon I read about in 1 Kings 11. Was this his ideal and the other the reality? Did he reform and change his approach to life at the end, and the historian who wrote Kings just neglected to tell us about it? I don't know, but I've known of other people who could preach a good sermon and give good advice but couldn't live up to their own words.

> ¹A good name is better than precious ointment; and the day of death than the day of one's birth. ²It is better to go to the house of mourning, than to go to the house of feasting: for that is the end of all men; and the living will lay it to his heart. ³Sorrow is better than laughter: for by the sadness of the countenance the heart is made better. ⁴The heart of the wise is in the house of mourning; but the heart of fools is in the house of mirth. ⁵It is better to hear the rebuke of the wise, than for a man to hear the song of fools. ⁶For as the crackling of thorns under a pot, so is the laughter of the fool: this also is vanity. ⁷Surely oppression maketh a wise man mad; and a gift destroyeth the heart. ⁸Better is the end of a thing than the beginning thereof: and the patient in spirit is better than the proud in spirit. ⁹Be not hasty in thy spirit to be angry: for anger resteth in the bosom of fools. ¹⁰Say not thou, What is the cause that the former days were better than these? for thou dost not enquire wisely concerning this. (Eccles. 7:1-10)

column prefer the older ways of doing things. When you look at society's attitudes and prevailing thought patterns or its readiness to accept sins that were considered shameful a mere generation or two ago, then this would be true. It is also true that more and more Biblical principles are being rejected today.

But simply focusing on the past and longing for "the good old days when life was simpler" will not solve any of our problems. God has placed us in this world to be a light and salt to the world. We cannot fulfill that purpose by becoming recluses. That tends to cut us off from the very people who need our help the most. Rather than living in the past, we should get out our Bibles and look at today—what is right and what is wrong now? By focusing on the "good old days" we may be missing some serious issues that we need to face today. Or some ways that God could use to promote the Gospel.[2]

Bible principles are timeless. Much of the direction in the New Testament is given in the form of Bible principles. These never change. But we live in a world that does change. We could make a whole list of items that are common today but have been invented within the last 150 years. For instance, motorized vehicles, airplanes, telephones,

---

[2] We can learn from illustrations of how serious believers of the past faced life and temptation. We can look at men like Rechab and Jehonadab (2 Kings 10) for an example of how keeping our families separated from the world helps them grow into righteous adults. But we can't just replicate the past and expect that to take care of today's issues.

electricity, computers, Internet, radios, television, and plastic were all invented during this time frame. We can't escape the influences of these inventions simply by deciding we will reject all of them. But we can go to the Bible for guidance on how to use them to God's glory.[3]

The person making the wise choices described in the first nine verses of this chapter is ready to face today's issues and choices. He can live and follow God's direction today.

Wisdom Is a Good Thing (7:11-22)

In the rest of chapter 7, Solomon shared various observations about wisdom and man. Solomon did some good thinking in this passage. We'll look at several of his observations:

Wisdom is good (11–15): I don't think Solomon is saying here that wisdom is great if you have lots of money. Instead, he is giving a contrast. Wisdom is like money, in that it will protect you and preserve your life. But having wisdom is not going to guarantee we will have an easy time in life. Nor does it guarantee long life. In fact, as Solomon noted in verse 15, the opposite can be true—a wise man may die young and a wicked man may live to a ripe old age. But in the end, wisdom is still an advantage because it helps us accept what God sends our way.

> [11]Wisdom is good with an inheritance: and by it there is profit to them that see the sun. [12]For wisdom is a defence, and money is a defence: but the excellency of knowledge is, that wisdom giveth life to them that have it. [13]Consider the work of God: for who can make that straight, which he hath made crooked? [14]In the day of prosperity be joyful, but in the day of adversity consider: God also hath set the one over against the other, to the end that man should find nothing after him. [15]All things have I seen in the days of my vanity: there is a just man that perisheth in his righteousness, and there is a wicked man that prolongeth his life in his wickedness. (Eccles. 7:11-15)

God is in control of life's circumstances. He may give us a crooked road to travel or a straight one. The wise person will accept what God has mapped out for him. God sends both prosperity and adversity. It is fine to rejoice in prosperity when God sends it, but adversity has

---

[3] This doesn't mean that we will accept every invention that comes along. For instance, we do not have a television in our home because the majority of programs on television are either harmful or unprofitable.

some advantages as well. It teaches us to think about life and its realities. It shows us that life is in God's hands, and it is not in our power to manipulate our future.

Wisdom avoids extremes (16–22): These verses have long intrigued me. First, we know it is good to be righteous and wise. Solomon himself wrote that elsewhere in Ecclesiastes and Proverbs. But here he says you should be careful not to overdo it, or you might destroy yourself. The NET translation renders this as "you might be disappointed." That seems a bit of a paradox.

> [16]Be not righteous over much; neither make thyself over wise: why shouldest thou destroy thyself? [17]Be not over much wicked, neither be thou foolish: why shouldest thou die before thy time? [18]It is good that thou shouldest take hold of this; yea, also from this withdraw not thine hand: for he that feareth God shall come forth of them all. [19]Wisdom strengtheneth the wise more than ten mighty men which are in the city. [20]For there is not a just man upon earth, that doeth good, and sinneth not. [21]Also take no heed unto all words that are spoken; lest thou hear thy servant curse thee: [22]For oftentimes also thine own heart knoweth that thou thyself likewise hast cursed others. (Eccles. 7:16-22)

Probably most people have heard the adage about people who were so heavenly minded that they were no earthly good. I can think of people who seem so perfect and sinless that you can hardly relate to them. For instance, I remember a minister telling his audience how he knelt beside his bed when he was eighteen years old and asked God to take away his problems with his temper. He stated that he had never struggled with his temper since then (about forty or fifty years later).

Solomon stated in verse 20 that all humans will be imperfect. When we expect perfection of people and don't accept them as God made them or how far God has brought them on their spiritual journey, we can cause them to be seriously discouraged. We can even be the cause of turning them away from Christ. Any person (such as the minister in the last paragraph) who states that he no longer struggles with sin is only fooling himself. Such people tend to have "weaknesses" and "failures" rather than sins.

Expecting perfection of ourselves can cause similar issues. If we fail to accept ourselves as humans who will fail because we are human, we open the door wide for Satan's accusations. This doesn't mean that we just expect to live in sin. But it does mean we will not wallow in defeat if we fail. If God forgives us, we should too. We will be human until the day we die, and we need to accept that.[4]

The second main statement in this passage is even harder to understand. You shouldn't be too wicked or foolish. (So a bit is okay?) Note that you might die before your time if you are. The Bible, in both the New and Old Testaments, warns against deliberate sins, or sins unto death.[5]

Perhaps Solomon was thinking along the same line. God has always made a difference between premeditated, deliberate sin and sins of ignorance. Even sins of impulse, where a person stumbles and falls, then gets up and continues in the Christian life, are different from deliberate sins where the person purposely continues living in his sinfulness.

It could also be that Solomon was simply stating this in natural terms, from a human perspective. People who are self-righteous are as obnoxious as people who glory in their sin. He ends up by saying that if we fear God, we should avoid both extremes. This was good advice, whether for Solomon's Old Testament peers or for the Christian today.

The Failure of Wisdom (7:23-29)

Earlier in this book, I mentioned that Solomon thought that whoever was in control of the universe and life had a "scheme" of some sort— some hidden plan or purpose. In these verses, he returned to this thought. He looked back over the process of his life as portrayed in Ecclesiastes and noted how he had tried his best to uncover the blueprint of life, but failed. He still seemed to think that it existed, but it was too "far off"— beyond human comprehension—and too deep for him to fathom.

---

[4] I know this paragraph will make some people squirm, and I don't want to carry these ideas to an extreme. But if we follow God, His grace will work in us to make us what He wants us to be. We need to do our part in avoiding temptations, etc., but finally, we depend on God for our salvation, not our own perfection. Study Titus 3:1-9 and Ephesians 2:1-10 for a balanced presentation on this subject.

[5] See Leviticus 4, 5; Numbers 15; 1 John 5:16, 17; etc.

But he did apply himself to the question of how wisdom fit into the scheme or blueprint of life, as well as folly and foolishness. His observations fit well with his writings in Proverbs about the strange woman and the foolish youth who fell into her snares.[6]

I have never heard a sermon on verse 28 of this chapter. Did Solomon really believe that men were morally superior to women? Perhaps his observations were tainted somewhat by his personal experience in dealing with a thousand women.

Solomon did make one astute observation here which probably came closer to the blueprint he was looking for than he realized. God created man (and woman) upright. The human problems of folly and sin were not God's fault—they were the result of man's deliberate choice to follow his own scheme of life rather than God's blueprint.[7] This has made an enormous problem for all mankind—people are caught in a quagmire of sin.[8] Too often they mistake wisdom for foolishness, and foolishness and folly for wisdom.[9]

God's blueprint has an answer for sin, folly, and foolishness. However, God didn't reveal the complete details of that blueprint until almost a thousand years after Solomon died. He did reveal enough to Solomon and others, however, that they could find their way to Him if they wanted to.

---

[6] See Proverbs 7:21-27, etc.

[7] The word *inventions* in verse 29 is often translated "schemes."

[8] Read Romans 1:21-32 for the New Testament's description of this.

[9] See 1 Corinthians 2:14.

FOR DISCUSSION

Read Ecclesiastes 7:1-29

Prelude

In this imaginary scene, the author depicts Solomon in an introspective mood. As he looked back over his life he felt a sense of gloom. This gloom often shines through as we read Ecclesiastes.

1. What are some things that may have caused Solomon's gloom, or sadness?

2. We tend to think in terms of right versus wrong or good versus bad. Why is it sometimes necessary to evaluate our choices in terms of good versus best or okay versus better?

Contrasts Illustrating Wisdom

Spend some time evaluating the chart in this section.

3. Compare the choices given for each of these rows in the chart. Why is the second choice better than the first one? Do you disagree with any? Why?

4. Some people like new things and are always ready to buy the latest electronic gadget. Others hate new things and the further away they can stay from them, the better. In what ways can each of these be a good thing? In what ways can they be unwise?

Wisdom Is a Good Thing

Solomon continues to use contrasts in this section to illustrate his thoughts.

5. In what ways is wisdom like money?

6. How do adversity and prosperity offset each other? Why is this good?

7. How can we be overly righteous? Or overly wicked? How can we avoid both extremes?

The Failure of Wisdom

Even the wisest, godliest, most intelligent, and highest-educated people stumble sometimes. All people are finite and will fail at times. None of us are wise enough to uncover everything God has placed in this world.

8. God made man and woman upright, but very few are upright today. What happened? What are the "evil inventions" Solomon mentioned in verse 29? (Note that this word is often translated "schemes.")

9. What does God's "blueprint" consist of? How (and why) do we know more about it than Solomon was able to find out?

PART THREE

Looking Beyond Vanity

———

Chapter 8 marks what seems to be another turning point in the book of Ecclesiastes. In this chapter, Solomon looked more closely at God, comparing God to an earthly king, and ended up proclaiming the impossibility of understanding God or His ways. From here on Solomon is on the homestretch, having accepted the fact that God is real and interacts with men. God still seemed somewhat distant to Solomon, but the relationship between him and God seemed to be growing.

Of God and Men

13

The fear of the LORD is the beginning of wisdom. Proverbs 9:10

Prelude

It had been many years since Solomon had felt intimidated by another man. He had intimidated many others, especially as he grew older and his temper grew shorter, but he had seldom been intimidated by someone else. Especially not when he was sitting on his throne with his guards on both sides of him.

This was different however.

He looked at the prophet again. He wasn't particularly appealing to look at. His hair was unkempt, and his robe was ragged. Even his sandals had seen better days. But his eyes caught and held Solomon's attention. They seemed to glow with a fierce inner light.

Their eyes locked for a moment or two, but Solomon looked away first. He felt foolish for his feelings. He could have this man removed with the wave of a hand. His guards were watching him for the signal to move in on him. But Solomon couldn't make himself do it.

The prophet simply stood there, apparently waiting for a response from Solomon. His steady gaze disconcerted him, and he started to become irritated. "Don't you know that I'm the king?" Solomon's voice was a little sharper than he had intended, but the prophet didn't cringe.

"I serve a King who is mightier than you," he answered calmly. "What answer shall I take back to Him?"

Solomon squirmed a little. "Tell Him that I have heard His message."

The prophet's gaze held him captive. "He will want to know how you plan to respond."

Solomon just wanted this standoff to end, but he didn't know what to say. He dropped his eyes to the prophet's sandals and noted that one of the thongs was torn. It had already been knotted once and would soon need to be fixed again, unless the prophet wanted to go barefooted.

He forced his mind back to the present. "Tell Him . . . tell Him that I will think on what you have told me." It annoyed him that his voice shook. He sighed with relief, almost audibly, when the prophet acknowledged his answer with a slight bow, turned, and strode from the audience chamber.

"Close the door behind him," he said to the guard at the doorway. "If anyone else is waiting to see me, tell them to come back tomorrow." He hesitated before adding, "I need some time alone to think." He seldom explained his actions to his guards, but they stood at attention, waiting until he had left the room before they looked at each other.

Solomon was ready to start his third theme in Ecclesiastes. His first picture had been almost incoherent, painted with brilliant but clashing colors. It especially portrayed his frustration with a life that had gotten out of his control. He liked logical, sensible conclusions, like the ones he had written in Proverbs when he was younger. But life wasn't like that anymore. Something had changed, and he suddenly realized that his life was ending. Even though he was the king and his word was law, it would mean nothing when he died.

His first word picture illustrated his anger at a life that made no sense in the light of death. I think it may even have shown us his anger toward the God he had drifted away from.

His second picture was more coherent but also drabber. It had some brilliant bursts of color here and there, but the effect still wasn't very pleasing. It spoke about the "inevitables" of life, the things that even a king couldn't change. He had calmed down, and his anger and frustration had faded, but the picture was still joyless. Shouldn't a man in his situation be joyous in his relation to the God who had done so much for him?

Solomon realized that at one point in his life he had possessed that joy. But it had faded away—like the sun fades behind the clouds on a dreary fall day.

It was time to tear the second picture from his easel. He would try again.

A King's Authority Is Absolute (8:1-9)

I can imagine Solomon sitting at his working table thinking about God. *So what is God really like? How can I explain God? What can I use to illustrate God to people who read this book?*

He started by talking about what it was like to be a king. He had lots of experience with that. And from his perspective, being God and being a king were similar in many ways. We

¹Who is as the wise man? and who knoweth the interpretation of a thing? a man's wisdom maketh his face to shine, and the boldness of his face shall be changed. ²I counsel thee to keep the king's commandment, and that in regard of the oath of God. ³Be not hasty to go out of his sight: stand not in an evil thing; for he doeth whatsoever pleaseth him. ⁴Where the word of a king is, there is power: and who may say unto him, What doest thou? ⁵Whoso keepeth the commandment shall feel no evil thing: and a wise man's heart discerneth both time and judgment. ⁶Because to every purpose there is time and judgment, therefore the misery of man is great upon him. ⁷For he knoweth not that which shall be: for who can tell him when it shall be? ⁸There is no man that hath power over the spirit to retain the spirit; neither hath he power in the day of death: and there is no discharge in that war; neither shall wickedness deliver those that are given to it. ⁹All this have I seen, and applied my heart unto every work that is done under the sun: there is a time wherein one man ruleth over another to his own hurt. (Eccles. 8:1-9)

don't think of it that way because we tend to have a different perspective of God than Solomon had.

Throughout history, most people thought of gods as powerful beings who needed to be appeased so they would be nice to you. Gods had a real advantage over people, just like kings did. If they didn't like you or if you offended them, you had better look out. Gods and kings didn't need to answer to anyone—they had the final word. If they decided to get even with you, you had no second court of appeal.

The best way to please a king was to do what he told you. Never sneak away when he wants you to do some work for him and don't challenge him. Do what you are told even if you don't agree with it or would prefer doing something else. It seems that Solomon assumed this was true of God as well.

I wonder how much his wives' heathen gods had rubbed off on Solomon. Did he just view God as a more powerful version of Ashtoreth? This would answer some of the questions that come up with Solomon's concluding chapters in Ecclesiastes.

He did go on and show some ways that God was different from a king. A king was human and subject to the frailties of humanity. He also had no power over death or his destiny—or over anyone else's destiny for that matter. And there was no way for a man to bail out from under God's authority and power.

Translations differ on their renderings of verse 9. The uncertainty centers on whether the king rules over other people to *their hurt* or to *his own hurt*. The difference isn't crucial, but he could be insinuating here that a king may be judged by God about how he treats others. Or he might be saying that a king has the authority to hurt those he rules over and God can do the same. I would lean toward the latter, but we can't really know for certain. Either interpretation could fit into the context here.

Life Will Not End Well for the Wicked (8:10-13)

About an hour south of Calgary, you can see a cluster of crosses at the edge of the road. Several years ago, a young man accosted his ex-girlfriend in a bar one evening and warned her that "this night will not end well for you." Later that night he forced her car off the road and shot four people, including her, with a high-powered rifle. Then he killed himself.

In recent years, this has become a common scenario. Kill some people—then, after you have gotten the attention you were after, kill yourself so you can avoid the consequences of your wrongdoing. This seems foolproof, *if you are sure this is where it all ends.* But what if it isn't?

> [10]And so I saw the wicked buried, who had come and gone from the place of the holy, and they were forgotten in the city where they had so done: this is also vanity. [11]Because sentence against an evil work is not executed speedily, therefore the heart of the sons of men is fully set in them to do evil. [12]Though a sinner do evil an hundred times, and his days be prolonged, yet surely I know that it shall be well with them that fear God, which fear before him: [13]But it shall not be well with the wicked, neither shall he prolong his days, which are as a shadow; because he feareth not before God. (Eccles. 8:10-13)

Solomon had complained earlier about life not being fair. He had pointed out that sometimes good people faced bad circumstances and bad people had it good. It didn't seem right to him that God didn't do something about it. Good people should be rewarded, and wicked people should be punished, he thought. People should know they couldn't get away with a wicked lifestyle.

In this passage Solomon gave another illustration of this but came to a different conclusion. He had seen wicked people entering the temple and later boasting about getting away with it. These same people even received honorable burial when they died, as if they had lived good lives. Solomon observed all this, but instead of talking about the unfairness of it, he seemed to remember that life doesn't end when you die and factored that into his thinking.

He didn't say why he changed his mind, but he was quite positive about his conclusion. It didn't matter how often the sinner got away with his sin or how good his life seemed to be. It still wasn't going to be well with him in the end. Since Solomon was sticking with observable data in this book, he didn't go into the eternal repercussions, but it seems evident that this must have been what he was thinking about. It *will not be well* with the wicked in the long run. It *will be well* for the people who fear God and live their lives like He wants.

This was a major shift in Solomon's thinking. No longer was he calling God unfair. He had nothing to say about the unfairness of life. Instead, he had begun to realize that these things would be straightened up in God's own timing. So what if things seemed to go well for the wicked. Judgment would rectify it.

Man Cannot Know God's Ways (8:14-17)

Solomon still didn't seem happy about the whole scenario, however, and says almost the same thing again. He still didn't like it that things seem unfair here and now. He had come to grips with the fact that all wrongs will be righted in the end. But he would have liked a more ideal solution—preferably one that took effect immediately.

In verse 15 Solomon slipped back to his old conclusion. Just eat, drink, and be merry while you live. Try to enjoy life within the circumstances that God has given you. But he seemed to realize that this was somewhat of a lame solution and put some more thought into it in the next verses.

His final solution in this chapter is a better one. You know, no matter how wise you are, you will never understand all God's ways in this life. Solomon realized he had overstepped his abilities. He was a wise man, an intellectual giant of

¹⁴There is a vanity which is done upon the earth; that there be just men, unto whom it happeneth according to the work of the wicked; again, there be wicked men, to whom it happeneth according to the work of the righteous: I said that this also is vanity. ¹⁵Then I commended mirth, because a man hath no better thing under the sun, than to eat, and to drink, and to be merry: for that shall abide with him of his labour the days of his life, which God giveth him under the sun. ¹⁶When I applied mine heart to know wisdom, and to see the business that is done upon the earth: (for also there is that neither day nor night seeth sleep with his eyes:) ¹⁷Then I beheld all the work of God, that a man cannot find out the work that is done under the sun: because though a man labour to seek it out, yet he shall not find it; yea farther; though a wise man think to know it, yet shall he not be able to find it. (Eccles. 8:14-17)

his time, and he had assumed he could figure out all of this. But Solomon had been humbled. God's ways were beyond his understanding.

Job came to the same conclusion at the end of the book of Job. God told him that he was darkening counsel by words without knowledge. And Job realized he needed to repent of his brashness. Do you think God was listening to Solomon and thinking the same thing about him?

FOR DISCUSSION

Read Ecclesiastes 8:1-17

Prelude

We do not know how God sent His last message to Solomon, but according to 1 Kings 11, He did send one. God normally used a prophet to communicate with David, so He may have done the same in this case. On the other hand, God appeared to Solomon the first two times in a dream, so He may have done that again. The method is not as important as the message.

1. From what you know of Solomon's history, why do you think he had lost the joy he once had in serving God? How might you lose your joy?

A King's Authority Is Absolute

As king, Solomon had absolute authority in Israel. As God, God has absolute authority over the earth and the universe, far surpassing Solomon's sphere of influence.

2. In what ways is it helpful to compare God with an earthly king, especially one who ruled in ancient times? In what ways are they different from each other?

3. How does Solomon's view of God in this section differ from yours?

Life Will Not End Well for the Wicked

From our viewpoint, it would seem fairer to have the incongruences of life squared away now rather than needing to wait for eternity.

4. How could Solomon be sure that in the end God would see to it that the wicked would get their due and the righteous would be vindicated?

5. Why might God choose to wait for eternity to set things right for both good and bad people? Is this always the case?

Man Cannot Know God's Ways

Solomon still seemed to like his earlier solution to life's dilemma: Eat, drink, and be merry.

6. Read Luke 12:13-21. What are the weaknesses of this solution to life's quandaries?

7. Read 1 Corinthians 1:18-31. Why would this passage have been hard for Solomon to accept? Is it hard for you to accept? Why or why not?

Life Is for Today

14

For I know the thoughts that I think toward you, saith the LORD, thoughts of peace, and not of evil, to give you an expected end. Jeremiah 29:11

Prelude

Solomon was sitting by his fireplace this evening. Instead of working, he was gazing into the fire, watching the flames dancing joyously. But for some reason, the sight depressed him.

He sighed and finally admitted the truth to himself. "I'm lonely. Here I sit, the richest and most powerful man in this part of the world, and I have no one to talk to."

It wasn't a happy thought. He had dozens of servants but no friends. He had a thousand wives but no one who loved him. Or was there? He thought back over the years, and finally a name came to him.

Naamah. His first wife. He hadn't seen her for months or talked to her for years. Yet at one time she had been his closest friend. In fact, he knew he had loved her and she had loved him.

"I wonder if she would spend the evening with me," he asked himself.

"Just to talk about when we were young. Has it been too long to revive what we once had?"

He went to the doorway and called his servant, who came immediately. "Go to the women's house and ask if Naamah would spend the evening with me." His servant blinked a little at this, but didn't comment. Solomon didn't usually ask women if they wanted to come and be with him. He simply told them to.

Solomon felt a little strange. He had almost forgotten that Naamah existed. But somehow, this evening, he felt a need to bring her into his life again.

Someone tapped at his door, breaking into his reverie.

But it wasn't who he had expected. His servant ushered in the matron of the women's house. Both looked a little uneasy, but the matron was never one to avoid a touchy subject.

"Naamah refused to come," the matron told him. Her eyes were on Solomon's face, and when he didn't respond she continued. "She said I'm to tell you that you are twenty years too late. The friendship is gone and it can't be rekindled, she said. She just wants to be left alone to die in peace."

It seemed as if the matron would have liked to say more, but she didn't. The sympathy in her eyes stung Solomon almost as much as her words had. But he realized that what Naamah had said was true. Some things even a king couldn't change. He turned to watch the flames again, hoping the matron hadn't seen the hurt in his face.

Finally he turned back to the waiting matron and spoke slowly. "Tell her I understand. I will leave her in peace." The matron must have been holding her breath because he heard her sigh with relief at his words.

She turned to leave, then turned back again. "I'm sorry," she whispered. Then she was gone.

Over and over in his writing, Solomon returned to thinking about the future. I did an analysis of Ecclesiastes early in my writing process and classified each of his questions. Of the thirty-two questions I came up with, twelve dealt with the future.

In this passage, Solomon again returned to this subject. He was still thinking about it—just musing out loud, you might say. He didn't have any real answers yet, but the frustration is gone from his writing. His painting is more peaceful now, and the colors are more harmonious.

Death Comes to All (9:1-6)

Solomon started right in with a thesis statement in this passage. The future is unknown to man, but the deeds of the righteous and the wise are in God's hands. Everything else in this passage should be understood in light of this statement.

Many of the conclusions he comes to in this passage are similar to statements he made earlier in the book. You will die, whether you

- are righteous or wicked,
- are good or evil,
- are clean or unclean,
- sacrifice or don't sacrifice,
- are a good person or a sinner,
- swear an oath or refuse to swear an oath.

The righteous and wise will not be spared death and the sorrow that goes with it. Just like the wicked, they will die. They may suffer from a long illness, or they may die quickly because of an accident. They may die of old age, or they may die young in the full blossom of youth. This is the end of all living beings and can't be avoided.

Any decisions or changes in life need to be made while you are still living because once you are dead, your fate is sealed. That is why Solomon said it's better to be a living dog than a dead lion. A living dog still has hope, but the dead lion is dead. His glory is gone, and his choices and accomplishments are past.

Again, as I said before, Solomon apparently limited himself to

> ¹For all this I considered in my heart even to declare all this, that the righteous, and the wise, and their works, are in the hand of God: no man knoweth either love or hatred by all that is before them. ²All things come alike to all: there is one event to the righteous, and to the wicked; to the good and to the clean, and to the unclean; to him that sacrificeth, and to him that sacrificeth not: as is the good, so is the sinner; and he that sweareth, as he that feareth an oath. ³This is an evil among all things that are done under the sun, that there is one event unto all: yea, also the heart of the sons of men is full of evil, and madness is in their heart while they live, and after that they go to the dead. ⁴For to him that is joined to all the living there is hope: for a living dog is better than a dead lion. ⁵For the living know that they shall die: but the dead know not any thing, neither have they any more a reward; for the memory of them is forgotten. ⁶Also their love, and their hatred, and their envy, is now perished; neither have they any more a portion for ever in any thing that is done under the sun. (Eccles. 9:1-6)

observable data—evidence that any thinking person could gather and analyze. He brought us to death's door numerous times in his writing, but seldom cracked the door open to give even a glimpse of what was on the other side. It could be that Solomon didn't know what was on the other side, or he may have been afraid of it. Or perhaps God wanted this book to be one that could be read by skeptic and believer alike.

No matter which was true, being good didn't bring any special favors with it. The good person could get a cold as easily as the sinner did. And both might die of cancer. It is good to live a healthy life, and that may make a difference in your death, but a sinner can live a healthy life as easily as a good person.

A person can, however, do something that will make life more worthwhile. We'll come back to that in the next chapter. In the meantime, these facts don't need to make us miserable. We can find joy in life despite its uncertainties.

Enjoy Life with the One You Love (9:7-10)

In the beginning of Ecclesiastes, it seemed that thinking about death and the future frustrated Solomon to the point that he lost all enjoyment in life. Apparently he had now come to grips with some of that. Earlier he had recommended a "wine, women, and song" approach to get your thoughts off the uselessness of life. This isn't a repeat of that, despite the similarities at first glance. Here he seems to be talking about the idea of counting your blessings and enjoying them.

All the ideals listed here are good for us today. First, be grateful that God has met your needs, and enjoy the food and drink which He has provided. These are simple pleasures that can be enjoyed by a good person or a sinner alike. But normally the good person, who will thank God for what he is enjoying, gets more joy and pleasure from it. The sinner tends to grump because he must eat rice instead of potatoes, or beans instead of beef. So thankfulness makes life worth living. I think Solomon saw this from his own experiences.

He added a little phrase at the end of verse 7 that people tend to overlook: "For God now accepteth thy works." In other words, God approves of what we are doing. We don't need to feel guilty about enjoying life and the pleasures God has given us. God's approval on our lives is worth more than anything else. If we have that, we have everything.

We could paraphrase the next verse (v. 8) like this: "Wear clean clothing and comb your hair." If you are a child of God, don't walk around looking as if you had lost your last friend! Smile at your neighbors and wave at the people you meet on the road. Don't dress like a tramp or wear shirts with stupid slogans on the chest. Act your part—God approves of you.

I think the next thought must have tugged at Solomon's heart, as I tried to show in the prelude introducing this chapter. Early in the writing process of this book, one of my reviewers raised the question about Solomon being lonely. I thought about that idea for a while and even ran it past a few people. Could a man with a thousand

> [7]Go thy way, eat thy bread with joy, and drink thy wine with a merry heart; for God now accepteth thy works. [8]Let thy garments be always white; and let thy head lack no ointment. [9]Live joyfully with the wife whom thou lovest all the days of the life of thy vanity, which he hath given thee under the sun, all the days of thy vanity: for that is thy portion in this life, and in thy labour which thou takest under the sun. [10]Whatsoever thy hand findeth to do, do it with thy might; for there is no work, nor device, nor knowledge, nor wisdom, in the grave, whither thou goest. (Eccles. 9:7-10)

wives be lonely? Really? Wouldn't he also have had lots of children? How could he be lonely?

I finally concluded that a man with a thousand wives would have to be lonely. One wife whom you love is one thing; but you can't love a thousand women like you love one. If you have a thousand wives, chances are you won't really love any of them. I'm guessing that at one time Solomon had a wife whom he really loved. His son Rehoboam was born the year before Solomon was crowned king, and he didn't marry his second wife until a few years after his coronation. This means he had three or four years with the wife of his youth[1] before the distractions started. If I know human nature at all, he often wished he could return to the early years of his marriage to his first wife.

That was his advice here. Live joyfully with the wife you love. Or if you're a woman, live joyfully with the man you love. Don't look around for someone better, someone prettier, someone more cheerful, someone not as bossy, or for all the other reasons that people get led astray. You know what? That second woman will be just as common, just as human, and just as moody as your first wife ever was. So will the third one and the fourth one. Just like you, those other women can put on a good front. But marriage is all about daily life, and when you get into the nitty-gritty of daily life, it won't be any better than life with your real wife was. But by then it will be too late. Nothing will ever be the same again.

Live joyfully with the wife of your youth. Jesus clarifies in the New Testament that God's will is for a marriage to be permanent. That won't be a hardship for you if your wife is the woman you love and she loves you. Unfortunately, that is almost a thing of the past in our society today. But God's children should be an example to the world, even in this.[2]

---

[1] In Proverbs 5:18, Solomon refers to rejoicing with the wife of your youth, and I have built on that in my illustration here.

[2] This isn't the time or place to pursue this further, but take a good look at what God's Word really says before making a rash decision to divorce your partner or marry someone who is divorced. Read Matthew 5:32 and 19:9 in their context for a start on this subject.

Searching for Meaning

Finally, one of the big things that helps make life worth living is putting yourself into it. If you're a farmer, be a good farmer. If you're a teacher, be the best teacher it is possible for you to be. If you're a writer, write the best books you can produce. If you're a mother, be a good mother, and if you're a father, be a good father. Mediocracy will never gain us any brownie points with anyone. Doing your best will please your boss, your spouse, your children, your neighbors—and God. And it will make you happy as well.

Remember, soon you will die. And once you are dead, your turn here is done. You will not get a second chance at life, despite what the Hindus teach about reincarnation. Once around the track is it. If you squander your one chance, you're done.[3]

I wonder if this is what Solomon was thinking about.

FOR DISCUSSION

Read Ecclesiastes 9:1-10

Prelude

The future and the past are tightly linked. The only thing separating them is that immeasurable moment called now.

1. The future is often a direct result of the past, but we tend to learn this too late. How is this true? Is it possible to change the future, even though we cannot change the past?

Death Comes to All

Death is inevitable. Whether we like the idea or not, death will catch up with all of us. We can either ignore it or prepare for it, but ignoring it will not make it go away.

2. This passage is a picture of life viewed from a naturalistic perspective. Why does this perspective tend to destroy meaning

---

[3] You can repent, however. Our God is merciful, and while we don't get a second chance around the track of life, repentance and forgiveness can clear the fog for us to find our way home.

in life? Who or what is missing in this perspective?

3. Naturalism is defined as *a belief that everything arises from natural properties and causes, with no supernatural or spiritual explanations for anything.* Is a naturalistic perspective of life more realistic than a spiritual perspective? Why or why not?

Enjoy Life with the One You Love

Love can be experienced by all humans, but a person whose heart is not turned toward God can realize only part of the perspective that love gives to life.

4. Do you agree with this statement? Why or why not?

5. Solomon collected women like some men collect stamps. How does an attitude like this destroy meaning in life?

6. In Ephesians 5:22-33, Paul used marriage as a type of Christ and the church. How was Paul's view of love different from Solomon's? How was it the same?

7. This passage states that "God now accepteth thy works." How should this concept affect our daily life? How does this bring meaning to life?

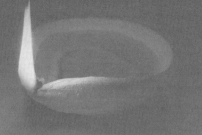

Wisdom Is Its Own Reward 15

Happy is the man that findeth wisdom . . . she is a tree of life to them that lay hold upon her: and happy is every one that retaineth her. Proverbs 3:13, 18

Prelude

Solomon was on a mission. One look at his worktable would have told you that. At first glance it seemed as if he had piled half his library on it. And the determination mirrored on his face would have told you the same thing.

Right now he was looking through one of the scrolls of his earlier writings.

"I wrote a lot about wisdom." He stroked his beard, a sure indicator that he was deeply involved in his thoughts. "I was sure confident back in those days." He read a few lines before stopping again. "Okay, so I should cry after knowledge. But I've done that—many times. I've searched for it as some people search for

Yea, if thou criest after knowledge, and liftest up thy voice for understanding; If thou seekest her as silver, and searchest for her as for hid treasures; Then shalt thou understand the fear of the lord, and find the knowledge of God. For the lord giveth wisdom: out of his mouth cometh knowledge and understanding. (Proverbs 2:3-6) *hidden treasures. And what good has it done?"*

He paused and read the next lines several times. "The Lord giveth wisdom . . ."
He let the scroll snap shut on its own accord. That wasn't really the answer
he wanted. He wanted something he could do, and do in a hurry.

He jumped to his feet and started pacing, pulling his beard at the same
time. "Is wisdom really just a gift from God? I know a lot of things, but
what really is wisdom? Is it something I can learn? Or do I just have to
wait for God to give it to me?"

Time was running out. Solomon could feel the signs in his body—the short-
ness of breath, the sleepless nights, the pains in his chest when he was under stress,
and even his short-temperedness. He needed answers, and he needed them soon.

This world contains a lot of foolishness. As you glance through the
headings in this chapter, you might wonder why I entitled the chapter
as I did. But the more you examine foolishness, the more grateful you
should be for any wisdom God has given you. Even a small amount of
wisdom can save you a lot of grief.

Wisdom is its own reward. As we consider various aspects of foolishness, keep that in mind. But first, let's follow Solomon's crooked trail
to consider a subject that bothers many people.

Wisdom and Chance (9:11, 12)

Christians are often uncomfortable with the concept of being lucky or
unlucky. I've even talked with people who don't care for the word "for-
tunate," though it has a slightly different tone than lucky.

Other people like to think they make their own luck. In other words,
the good things that happen to them are because of their hard work
or abilities. Usually they aren't as quick to take responsibility for their
"bad luck," but some might even go that far.

Some people believe in fate, or the sovereignty of God, where every
detail of life is laid out for them in advance and is totally out of their

control. If they are predestined to be a sinner, all their best attempts to repent or change their ways will be for naught.[1] Others believe the opposite. Everything that happens to them is just chance, whether it is bad, good, or indifferent.

So what did Solomon mean in this passage? We could probably take this several ways. My first inclination is to believe that he was simply writing from his observations again. Sometimes the rabbit wins the race, and sometimes the turtle wins. Of course, if you have read that old fable, you know that the turtle's wisdom and the rabbit's foolishness had as much to do with the turtle's victory as chance did. But if you had been at the finish line watching, you wouldn't have known that.

> [11]I returned, and saw under the sun, that the race is not to the swift, nor the battle to the strong, neither yet bread to the wise, nor yet riches to men of understanding, nor yet favour to men of skill; but time and chance happeneth to them all. [12]For man also knoweth not his time: as the fishes that are taken in an evil net, and as the birds that are caught in the snare; so are the sons of men snared in an evil time, when it falleth suddenly upon them. (Eccles. 9:11, 12)

Sometimes a skilled hunter may come home empty-handed despite his hunting experience. But the boy next door, who is in his first year of hunting, may get a nice big buck. I knew someone who took a nap while he was hunting. He woke up with a large buck standing almost in front of him. So he raised his rifle and shot it. The buck had the largest antlers of any shot in the province that year. Was that chance or skill? Or God's providence?

Similarly, smart men sometimes die bankrupt, and others who aren't as smart may leave a large inheritance because they "happened" to be at the right place at the right time.

When IBM, the largest computer company in the world, wanted to develop a new line of PCs, they went to see Digital Research since they had developed the main personal computer system in use at that

---

[1] We often call this belief Calvinism, even though it doesn't really reflect what Calvin or Augustine believed. Many Calvinists do not carry their beliefs to this degree, and we should be careful to find out what they actually mean when they say things that sound different from what we are used to hearing.

time. The owner of Digital Research wasn't at work that day, despite having made an appointment with them, so they talked to his wife instead. She didn't like the terms of their offer and sent them packing. Feeling rebuffed, IBM contacted a young university graduate called Bill Gates, who had a small startup company called Microsoft. "Sure," Gates replied. "No problem at all. Let's talk about it."

Today Digital Research no longer exists, and Microsoft is one of the world's largest companies. All because of that one incident. Sheer time and chance, right?

I'm not sure. Maybe God really didn't care whether Digital Research or Microsoft built IBM's new operating system. Or maybe He did; we simply don't know. But I don't think God necessarily micromanages the world. He won't keep you from making a poor choice, though He may require that you live through the consequences of that choice.

Here is another scenario. Close to twenty years ago, we moved from the eastern part of the continent to the western part. So far, as our children have grown up, they have married people they met here in the west and would probably not have met had we not moved. So suppose we hadn't moved west and our children had married people they met in the east. Would that have been God's plan for them? Or would they have needed to stay single? Or would God have somehow made sure that they got together with "the right person" anyway?

I don't think God micromanages things that way. I think our children married within God's will, and if we had stayed in the east, they could have been in God's will by marrying people they met there. So from Solomon's perspective, it was time and chance that brought my children their partners. But if you look behind the scenes, I think God had His hand in things as well.

Once I had to choose between two jobs. I could continue working for the company I was with but from a home office, or I could accept an offer from a Christian publisher to work for them. I wasn't sure what course to take, so I asked one of our ministers what I should do. He told me,

"Really, I don't care which you do." That startled me because I thought he would encourage me to work for the publisher. But I think sometimes God leaves it up to us, and any decision we make isn't necessarily right or wrong. This minister understood that. So I took the offer I got first and decided that was what God wanted me to do. And it worked out fine.

We should be as wise as we can in our choices. Circumstances will often give us some direction, but we don't need to agonize for hours and days over these things. If we're honestly seeking God's will, He is willing to bless our choice no matter which one we make.

And the person looking on may shake his head and say, "My, he was lucky that time." But we know that even time and chance can be controlled by God.

Wisdom Is Often Despised (9:13-16)

The people we consider important and often look up to aren't always the wise people. We have our preconceived ideas about what makes a person wise or how we can become wise ourselves. We tend to think that people who read complicated books and have learned a large vocabulary of specialized jargon are wise. We often look up to people like that, even if we might not understand what they are saying.

Many times we allow ourselves to be fooled by inflated egos and fail to heed the wisdom of the common people among us. For instance, I read about a tractor-trailer that was stuck under a bridge. The driver hadn't noticed the height warning and found himself solidly wedged under the bridge. People swarmed around with all kinds of suggestions. The tow truck driver was afraid he would pull the truck apart if he tried to pull it out, but no one could figure out what else to do. One person came up with the idea of jacking up the

13This wisdom have I seen also under the sun, and it seemed great unto me: 14There was a little city, and few men within it; and there came a great king against it, and besieged it, and built great bulwarks against it: 15Now there was found in it a poor wise man, and he by his wisdom delivered the city; yet no man remembered that same poor man. 16Then said I, Wisdom is better than strength: nevertheless the poor man's wisdom is despised, and his words are not heard. (Eccles. 9:13-16) bridge, but that would probably damage the bridge. Another person had another far-fetched idea. Finally a little boy who had been watching piped up, "Why don't you let the air out of the tires?"

It worked. The wisdom in this situation didn't come from the professionals. It took a little boy's idea to solve the dilemma.

I doubt that the little boy was appointed mayor the next day. He probably just went back to school. That is like the story Solomon gave in this passage. The point is that wisdom doesn't necessarily come from where we expect. And we can easily despise and overlook the wise people among us. They often aren't who we think they are.

Folly Can Outweigh Wisdom (9:17–10:1)

Verse 17 gives an interesting picture. Here you see a wise man giving quiet advice in the background, mostly unnoticed, at least by the crowd of fools. In the foreground, a foolish king is roaring orders to a noisy crowd. If people would be quiet, the wise man could give them good advice. But he isn't heard by most of them. The noise of the crowd and the bellowing of the king overrides it all.

> 17The words of wise men are heard in quiet more than the cry of him that ruleth among fools. 18Wisdom is better than weapons of war: but one sinner destroyeth much good. 1Dead flies cause the ointment of the apothecary to send forth a stinking savour: so doth a little folly him that is in reputation for wisdom and honour. (Eccles. 9:17–10:1)

One person can turn a situation around if we are willing to listen to his wisdom. On the other hand, one sinner or troublemaker can quickly undo the work of months. It can work both ways.

Folly can do a lot of damage. It doesn't take much folly to destroy wisdom. Because of this, even a wise person needs to be careful because he can destroy his usefulness very quickly if he allows folly in his life. A few flies in the perfume will ruin the whole jar. One failure can make people doubt everything you say. If it's serious, it may ruin your reputation for life.

I've heard various discussions about this subject. The point here is not whether this is right or wrong. It is, again, simply an observation on Solomon's part.

Foolish Authority Can Nullify Wisdom (10:2-7)

A fool is a lot different from a wise person. According to Solomon, you can even tell the difference by the way he walks, or perhaps where he walks. I think you can also tell by the way he talks or what he says. Abraham Lincoln said it like this: *"It is better to remain silent and be thought a fool, than to speak out and remove all doubt."* [2]

Solomon felt strongly about the contrast between wisdom and folly. He must have seen a lot of folly in his time. Folly wasn't isolated to his time however. Some of the statements people make, even to proclaim Christ, can sound foolish. I can remember experiences in my own life when I said such things. Oh, I meant well, but I didn't know as much as I thought I did. It is better to take the time to learn from wise people around us and those with more experience.

> [2]A wise man's heart is at his right hand; but a fool's heart at his left. [3]Yea also, when he that is a fool walketh by the way, his wisdom faileth him, and he saith to every one that he is a fool. [4]If the spirit of the ruler rise up against thee, leave not thy place; for yielding pacifieth great offences. [5]There is an evil which I have seen under the sun, as an error which proceedeth from the ruler: [6]Folly is set in great dignity, and the rich sit in low place. [7]I have seen servants upon horses, and princes walking as servants upon the earth. (Eccles. 10:2-7)

In 1848, Mrs. Cecil Alexander published a children's hymn entitled "All Things Bright and Beautiful." The third verse of this song went like this:

The rich man in his castle,
The poor man at his gate,
God made them high and lowly,
And ordered their estate.

Many people at that time would have considered this song to be accurate, that God predestined the estate of both the high and the lowly.[3]

---

[2] See also Proverbs 17:28.

[3] This verse has lost its popularity in modern society. In Canada, it is often replaced with, "The rocky mountain splendour, / the lone wolf's haunting call, / the great lakes and the prairies, / the forest in the fall."

During medieval times and earlier, most societies believed that God[4] decided your status in society by the family you were born into. If your father was a blacksmith, that was your future. If he was a farmer, you would be a farmer. If your family had noble blood, you were destined to be a nobleman. People who refused to live within the class God had chosen for them became misfits and outcasts.

Solomon could have been referring to such a scenario in the last verses of this passage. The idea of lower class people taking a high place and ruling over the wealthy and (supposedly) wiser people seemed ignominious to Solomon. Why would servants or slaves ride horses when their "superiors" had to walk?

This scenario has taken place more than once in history. The class revolutions in Russia and China both zeroed in on the wealthy and the intellectuals around them. Neither of these revolutions ended up improving society the way the perpetrators hoped it would. However, I don't think we should use this passage to portray that the Bible supports suppressing the poorer class. If this is the focus of Solomon's thoughts in this passage, it is merely the product of his worldview.

I think, rather, that Solomon was simply illustrating how easily folly can destroy the work of the wise or the wealthy. Solomon's observations show us a lot about people's natural tendencies. Folly can even move into a congregation of Christians and destroy the work of a generation in a year or two.

Foolishness Is Dangerous (10:8-11)

When a person digs a pit, will he automatically fall into it? Versions are divided on this question, with about half of them saying he will fall into it. The Septuagint agrees with this as well. But other versions translate this to say that the person who digs a pit *may* fall into it, which seems a reasonable reading.[5]

---

[4] Or the gods, depending on the society you were part of.

[5] See the textual notes in the NET version for more discussion of this.

Again, this passage can be taken various ways. Solomon may have been talking about a foolish neighbor, or even a foolish king, who was trying to harm someone by these actions. In that case, he was showing how easily vindictive actions can rebound and do us the harm that we wanted to bring on someone else. Foolish actions are dangerous, both to the perpetrator and the victim.

> [8]He that diggeth a pit shall fall into it; and whoso breaketh an hedge, a serpent shall bite him. [9]Whoso removeth stones shall be hurt therewith; and he that cleaveth wood shall be endangered thereby. [10]If the iron be blunt, and he do not whet the edge, then must he put to more strength: but wisdom is profitable to direct. [11]Surely the serpent will bite without enchantment; and a babbler is no better. (Eccles. 10:8-11)

On the other hand, he may just have been talking about using wisdom in our regular work. Safety precautions are wise, but fools do not pay any attention to danger. So the man digging a pit may end up falling into it and being hurt because he hasn't taken some common-sense precautions. The person cutting down a hedge should take precautions against poisonous snakes, especially if he knows that they are common in the area. If you are removing a stone wall, be aware that a rock could land on your foot, and if you're splitting firewood be careful so your axe doesn't slip and cut your leg.

Safety precautions are often as simple as using common sense. Naturally, it will take you longer to cut down a tree if your axe or your chainsaw is dull, and it is also more dangerous. But if you sharpen them before using them and put on some protective clothing or shoes, the situation changes dramatically.

Not taking such common-sense precautions is as foolish as thinking that a snake won't bite you before you charm it. And it is just as foolish to think you can babble all kinds of nonsense and not have to face the consequences.

Foolishness Self-Destructs (10:12-15)

Foolishness is foolish. I suppose that is obvious, but Solomon wanted to make sure he got his point across. I will list some of his thoughts here:

- Fools are destroyed by their own words. (v. 12)

- Fools base their words on foolish assumptions. (v. 13)

- The conclusions of a fool are wicked madness (almost every version uses a stronger word than "mischievous" to describe a fool's mad conclusions). (v. 13)

- Fools multiply words (keep on babbling, chatter on and on) even if they have no idea what they are talking about. (v. 14)

- Fools are so exhausted by their work that they get lost on the way home (workers lived in towns or cities, so this seems the logical meaning). (v. 15)

By now we can safely conclude that our words are a good indication of whether we are foolish or wise. Solomon may have used some exaggeration to make his point, but I think he made himself clear.

Are you wise? Listen to your words. And remember that "in the multitude of words there wanteth not sin: but he that refraineth his lips is wise" (Prov. 10:19).

Wisdom Is Threatened by Inexperience (10:16-20)

Foolishness and inexperience have a lot in common with each other. An inexperienced leader is going to have a lot of problems, whether he leads a country, a corporation, or a church. He won't know how to direct the people he is trying to lead and will probably end up letting them do as they please.

These verses mention princes who lack self-control. They feast in the morning and get drunk. Furthermore, they are lazy and things are falling apart around them. Parties are much more fun than doing the work necessary to make the kingdom run smoothly. Parties help you laugh, wine makes you happy, and money gets you anything you want—except wisdom. Because of this, the kingdom is going to collapse around the inexperienced king and his foolish followers like the proverbial house of cards.

This again could have been a veiled allusion to Solomon's son Rehoboam. He never comes out and says so directly. But he gives enough hints in Ecclesiastes that I suspect he wasn't happy with his son's potential to rule his kingdom wisely.

[16]Woe to thee, O land, when thy king is a child, and thy princes eat in the morning! [17]Blessed art thou, O land, when thy king is the son of nobles, and thy princes eat in due season, for strength, and not for drunkenness! [18]By much slothfulness the building decayeth; and through idleness of the hands the house droppeth through. [19]A feast is made for laughter, and wine maketh merry: but money answereth all things. [20]Curse not the king, no not in thy thought; and curse not the rich in thy bedchamber: for a bird of the air shall carry the voice, and that which hath wings shall tell the matter. (Eccles. 10:16-20)

The last verse in this passage seems to be a random thought that came to him—maybe a warning to the people who might want to take advantage of the king he has just talked about. Inexperienced or not, a king is no one to fool with. And the rich people who are taking advantage of him will be just as inclined to deal harshly with you as the king would.

Rebellious thoughts get around as if the birds of the air were spreading them. Don't think that you will be able to hide them. So be wise and keep your mouth shut, no matter how foolish others are acting.

Wisdom is its own reward. Let God give you His wisdom, and you will avoid much grief. Foolishness has its own reward too, but after reading this chapter, I think you realize that the reward of foolishness is not something you want to look for.

If any of you lack wisdom, let him ask of God, that giveth to all men liberally, and upbraideth not; and it shall be given him. (James 1:5)

FOR DISCUSSION

Read Ecclesiastes 9:11–10:20

Prelude

Wisdom is one of those things that tend to happen while we are thinking about something else. It is usually received somewhat indirectly—by hungering and thirsting after God and seeking to live in His will. If we go looking for it we probably won't find it. We can gain knowledge through studying and research, but that isn't normally how we get wisdom.

    1. According to James 1:5, how do you get wisdom? Is that the *only* way?

    2. What does Proverbs 2:3-6 add to this?

Wisdom and Chance

Sometimes what looks like chance to us is the result of someone's quiet wisdom. But other times what looks like wisdom may have just been chance. Other times it was neither, but was the result of God's overruling providence.

    3. If this passage is simply recording Solomon's observations, should we take it as truth? Does God overrule in small things that seem unimportant? Is it okay for the Christian to make decisions without receiving direct guidance from God?

    4. Maybe you can see God shrugging His shoulders about the IBM and Microsoft scenario. But what about the idea of God micromanaging who you or your children marry? Does God always overrule everyday happenings? Explain your answer.

    5. How does Proverbs 11:14 impact this discussion?

Wisdom Is Often Despised

Often, we don't recognize the wise people around us.

    6. What are some of the things that we mistake for wisdom? How can this be a problem?

7. What are some indicators of genuine wisdom? (Consider James 3:13-18.)

Folly Can Outweigh Wisdom

The quiet words of a wise man can accomplish more than the yelling of a fool.

8. Why do we tend to pay more attention to the noise of fools than to quiet words of wisdom?

9. How could a little folly destroy the reputation that a wise man has spent years developing?

10. Why do sin and folly have such a strong influence on people?

Foolish Authority Can Nullify Wisdom

Foolishness and wisdom are like oil and water; you can't mix them. They are diametrically opposed to each other.

11. What are some ways you can tell a foolish person from a wise person? What happens when a wise person allows foolishness into his life?

12. The concept of a classless society is new in history. How do some of the revolutions of the last century prove that folly can destroy wisdom?

Foolishness Is Dangerous

Fools consider foolishness to be fun. But too often the "fun" turns into something more serious.

13. When does "fun" become dangerous? Why?

14. In what ways does common sense equate with wisdom?

Foolishness Self-Destructs

This passage is like the last one. Foolishness may damage others, but it will damage the person who is doing it even more.

15. Why do fools tend to believe that what they say is true, even when it is obvious to those around them that it isn't? Why do fools often talk too much?

Wisdom Is Threatened by Inexperience

Sometimes we can't avoid being inexperienced in what we are doing. But we can find ways to keep this from doing damage.

16. Give some illustrations of situations where inexperience did a lot of damage to wisdom. How could this have been avoided?

17. Does experience always equal wisdom? Does wisdom always equal experience? Explain.

18. An inexperienced leader is often more dangerous than an experienced one. Why would this be the case?

19. What are the rewards of wisdom? How are they better than the rewards of foolishness?

Practical Advice About Life

16

It is good for a man that he bear the yoke in his youth. Lamentations 3:27

Prelude

Solomon was on his throne in the audience chamber when the messenger arrived. He was a young man, athletic and blond-haired. It was obvious by the worn appearance of his clothing that he had come a long way. He was carrying a packet of documents.

He bowed low before Solomon before speaking. "I bring you good tidings, O King. Your ships have returned safely from their voyage to the far west.[1] They are laden with many wonderful things, such as gold, silver, ivory, apes, and peacocks. I have the details of the cargo in this packet."

Solomon smiled. "Well done, my friend. Give the packet to my householder so he can go over the listing." He paused and motioned to a guard.

---

[1] Most commentators and translators take the reference to Tarshish to mean that these were large ships capable of traveling to Tarshish. Compare 1 Kings 10:22 with 1 Kings 22:48 where the ships were built on the coast of the Red Sea, obviously with the intent of going either to the east coast of Africa or the west coast of India.

"Take the messenger to the kitchen and give him food and wine, then find him a bed for the night. He has done well to bring us this good news."

It was easy to see that Solomon was pleased with the messenger's news. The journey to the west was fraught with danger and took three years to complete. It was always good news when the ships returned safely. Also, the cargo they brought was almost priceless. It would add a significant value to Solomon's treasury.

Solomon started into Ecclesiastes doubting God's influence on the universe and mankind. If he did believe in God, he wasn't very confident of His ability to manage His creation or His desire to do so.

But as you read through Ecclesiastes, you see this changing. His intellectual suppositions gradually gave way to faith. He began to realize that the God of his fathers was a benevolent being—One who was highly involved in the universe and mankind rather than a dictator who really didn't care what happened to His creation.

By the final chapter of Ecclesiastes Solomon seemed to have accepted that he would never change God or the way God ran His creation. We can't bend God to suit our fancies. Instead, it is wise to change our ways to fit God's direction. When we work within God's framework, things go much better.

Wisdom in the Face of an Unknown Future (11:1-6)

We face a lot of unknown things in life. The future is the greatest of these, and Solomon gave some ideas in this passage about facing the future. Taken in context, this passage seems to be speaking of practical ways to succeed in everyday life. These principles hold true in many other areas of life as well.

Bible teachers sometimes use the first verses of this chapter to teach the value of being generous to others. Normally they also add the promise that we will reap a good reward when we do this.

Others, however, infer that the first several verses speak of trade and investment. Both Kings and Chronicles note that Solomon sent ships to trade. So these verses could also apply to being ready to invest our money and efforts in business life. He advised caution because business can be risky, especially maritime business, where ships could easily be wrecked at sea or captured by pirates. Because of this, he sent several ships so that even if one or two didn't get back, the success of the others would help pay for their loss.

This principle could be useful in many ways. Farmers would be wise to diversify rather than depending on one source of income. Workers should be acquainted with several trades in case they lose their job and need to find work elsewhere. We don't know the future, so it is wise to be prepared.

At the same time, God has set certain natural laws in place for our safety. Certain kinds of clouds bring rain. When a tree falls, it doesn't change direction on the way down or move after it has fallen. So there are some certainties we can depend on.

> [1]Cast thy bread upon the waters: for thou shalt find it after many days. [2]Give a portion to seven, and also to eight; for thou knowest not what evil shall be upon the earth. [3]If the clouds be full of rain, they empty themselves upon the earth: and if the tree fall toward the south, or toward the north, in the place where the tree falleth, there it shall be. [4]He that observeth the wind shall not sow; and he that regardeth the clouds shall not reap. [5]As thou knowest not what is the way of the spirit, nor how the bones do grow in the womb of her that is with child: even so thou knowest not the works of God who maketh all. [6]In the morning sow thy seed, and in the evening withhold not thine hand: for thou knowest not whether shall prosper, either this or that, or whether they both shall be alike good. (Eccles. 11:1-6)

We need to be willing to take some risks in life. The farmer who never takes risks never gets a harvest. The businessman who never tries a new idea will probably never be successful. But in all that we need to remember that God is in control, and we don't understand His ways. Sometimes what seems a sure thing will turn into a failure. Or a risky venture might turn out to be a success. We must be willing to accept what God sends our way, because we simply can't see what is happening behind the scenes.

Solomon raised the subject of work ethics various times in Ecclesiastes, and it appears that he did so again in verse 6. Be at work early, and work late. You don't know which labor God will bless, so be willing to diversify. Work hard, and leave the results in God's hands.

Enjoy Life, But . . . (11:7, 8)

Solomon tried to tie together the loose ends of Ecclesiastes in chapter 11 before concluding with chapter 12. He was in the process of putting the finishing touches on his masterpiece. Now we can step back and look at his picture. The dull colors, the clashing colors, and the frustrating colors in the picture are starting to make sense and have become part of its overall beauty. Somehow, he has brought harmony to the whole.

Life will always include some futility (v. 8). But that is life. God has seen fit to give us enough good days to make life bearable. But He also gives us enough bad days that we realize how good the good days really are. Life has many simple pleasures if we view them from the right perspective.

If you view life from the perspective that Solomon portrayed in the beginning of the book, you will totally miss what God offers you. The joys of a job well done, the joys of marriage and family, the beauties of nature, the restfulness of a peaceful night's sleep, and the satisfaction of eating and drinking what God has provided for you are all part of what makes life worthwhile. Even the atheist and the agnostic can understand that.

At first, Solomon totally overlooked these things because he thought he could find satisfaction in his knowledge and his wealth and the pleasures that they could bring him. He found the praise of admirers like the Queen of Sheba gratifying to his ego. He was a successful man—he had done great things, and he knew it. He was a wise

> [7] Truly the light is sweet, and a pleasant thing it is for the eyes to behold the sun: [8] But if a man live many years, and rejoice in them all; yet let him remember the days of darkness; for they shall be many. All that cometh is vanity. (Eccles. 11:7, 8)

man, and he knew it. His intellectual knowledge of natural things and philosophical ideas surpassed that of anyone else, and he knew it. He had access to more women than any man could possibly want, and he knew it. He had *everything* a man could wish for—*except meaning in life*. And he knew that too.

Solomon didn't find meaning in his life from those things because they aren't what brings meaning to life. Meaning in life is found in accepting life as God gives it and enjoying the simple things He brings to us. Even a sick man on his deathbed can find meaning and joy in life by accepting God's will.

Maybe it's an oversimplification, but it seems that Solomon got his eyes off God and onto the glittering imitations that life offered him. Then he wondered where God had gotten to. How many times have you and I done the same thing? When God goes missing, we had better backtrack and figure out where we took a wrong turn and lost sight of Him. That was, at least partly, what Solomon was doing when he wrote Ecclesiastes.

But how much better it would have been had he not lost sight of God in the first place. God graciously accepts our repentance, but it is much better to live for Him as we go through life than to hope for the opportunity to repent at the end.

This is where Ecclesiastes 11 should end, so we will look at the rest of the passage in the next chapter.

FOR DISCUSSION

Read Ecclesiastes 11:1-8

Prelude

Wise as he was, Solomon almost made the fatal mistake of allowing foolishness to ruin his life.

1. Many of today's highly esteemed people fit into the earlier part of Ecclesiastes. If they believe in God at all, they consider

Him only as a vague influence in their lives. In what way did Solomon's perspective of God seem to change?

Wisdom in the Face of an Unknown Future

Life is full of uncertainties and insecurities. The wise man will do what he can to deal with these, then leave the future in God's hands.

2. Why is it wise at times to take risks in life? At what point does risk-taking become foolishness?

3. Do you feel uncomfortable with any of the principles suggested in this section? Why?

4. How could we adapt these same principles from a spiritual perspective?

5. If we want to find meaning in a world that often doesn't seem to make sense, we need to be willing to leave the future and the results of our lives in God's hands. Why?

Enjoy Life, But . . .

Longfellow once said that "Into each life some rain must fall." Storms are a part of every successful person's life. If no rain falls on an area, it soon becomes a lifeless desert.

6. A big part of finding meaning in life is our perspective of life. How did Solomon's perspective of life almost turn his life into a spiritual desert?

7. What are some of the simple joys in life that make life worthwhile? Is this enough to give us meaning in life? What else do we need?

8. What happens when God seems to be missing?

PART FOUR

Solomon's Conclusion— Fear God

In the last chapter of Ecclesiastes, Solomon drops his philosophical facade. He speaks directly to us about relating to the God he has redis-covered in his journey. His idea of relating to God is somewhat like he would expect his subjects to relate to him as king. This perspective seems lacking in warmth to us, but we live in a new dispensation— one where the relationship between man and God is more like the relationship between a father and his children. Try as we might, we don't really understand the perspective of the Old Testament, which in most cases was like subjects relating to their king.

Remember Your Creator in Your Youth

17

I have been young, and now am old. Psalm 37:25

Prelude

Solomon was old. He wasn't sure when it happened. But it had dawned on him one day while he was trying to describe how it felt to be old.

It was a deflating experience. But he should have known. He had just been avoiding the truth because he didn't want to admit it. His father had been only about ten years older than Solomon was now when he had given in to old age. But suddenly he knew—he wasn't sure how, but he did—that he would never become as old as his father.[1] He looked down at the pieces of papyri on his writing table. "I'm almost done," he told himself. "Just a few more hours to go. I might be able to finish tomorrow evening."

But in the meantime, he had better try to get some sleep. Sleep had

---

[1] Part of the reason for this could have been his luxurious and licentious lifestyle.

become precious the last while. It seemed that he was always tired, yet he could never sleep soundly when he did go to bed.

His steps dragged as he shuffled his way to his bed chamber. His servant had been waiting outside the door and heard him coming.

"You should have called me, Master," he scolded gently as he helped Solomon take the last few steps. "You might fall and hurt yourself."

Solomon trembled from exertion as he sat on the side of his bed. "You will soon be rid of me," he told his servant, ignoring the admonition. "I hope your next master is as good to you as you have been to me."

"No," the servant replied. "I will never find another master like you." He helped Solomon lie down and pulled the covers over him. Solomon often got cold at night.

He paused at the door. "Remember, I'm sleeping right out here. If you need anything, please call."

I spent several weeks in the hospital a while ago, and it taught me some lessons about life that were good for me. Someone once said that over the entry doors to every hospital they should put a sign stating, "Lose all dignity, you who enter here . . ."[2] You could say the same thing about old age, at least for many people.

Most young people do not understand the realities of old age. Solomon did, and he describes them in a poetical form that is almost unmatched by any other Bible passage.

Remember . . . (11:9–12:1)

The whole book of Ecclesiastes is introspective. Reminiscing is the privilege of old people, and Solomon was old. But Solomon also put in a special message for young people at the end of chapter 11 and

---

[2] A parody of the sign that Dante pictured as hanging over the gates of hell, stating, "Abandon all hope, ye who enter here." See "Inferno," Canto III, in Dante's epic poem entitled *Divine Comedy*. The statement above is intended to be tongue in cheek, but the original has nothing humorous about it.

the beginning of chapter 12. He remembered being young and how it felt. He probably realized that it was while he was young that he had planted the seeds that led him away from God. We don't have a time line for Ecclesiastes, but it would have taken years for everything he recounts in this book to have happened.

In our young years we often lay the groundwork for many of our problems in life. Most older people reading this book would doubtless agree with me. They have probably done their share of reminiscing as well. But youth is the time of life when we are full of zeal and have dreams for the future. This zeal can lead us into doing things that we will regret for a lifetime. So rejoice, young person. Be glad you are young and can enjoy life. Let your heart lead you. But remember—God is watching. He is glad you are enjoying life, but He is also keeping track. Someday you will give an account to Him for what you did.

> [9]Rejoice, O young man, in thy youth; and let thy heart cheer thee in the days of thy youth, and walk in the ways of thine heart, and in the sight of thine eyes: but know thou, that for all these things God will bring thee into judgment. [10]Therefore remove sorrow from thy heart, and put away evil from thy flesh: for childhood and youth are vanity. [1]Remember now thy Creator in the days of thy youth, while the evil days come not, nor the years draw nigh, when thou shalt say, I have no pleasure in them; (Eccles. 11:9--12:1)

Solomon mentioned judgment here, but we may need to face up to our mistakes before judgment. Solomon did. His mistakes and sins clouded what should have been a comfortable old age. His reminiscing included a lot of memories that I am sure he wished he could erase but couldn't.

Youth doesn't last long. The prime of life is soon gone. Before you know it, you too will face old age. Don't sow seeds of sorrow and sin while you are young, because they will trouble you when you are old. Instead, follow God and put Him first in your life. Life will take many twists and turns, but if you keep your eyes on God, He will take you safely through. He won't always give you what you want or let you go where you want to go, but if your goal is to serve Him, He will guide you and be with you. You will not need to seek meaning in life or wonder when God got off the train.

So think about God when you are young.[3] Think seriously about Him. Ask yourself what kind of memories you want to have when you are old. I know it is hard for young people to imagine themselves as being old, but try it anyway.

Furthermore, you may not get to old age.

Before . . . (12:2-7)

We could summarize 12:2-7 as saying, "Remember God before you are old, and can't." That is a chilling thought, isn't it? Earlier in Ecclesiastes Solomon mentioned that a tree would lie where it fell. Did you ever think of it that a tree will probably fall in the direction it is leaning? If you have leaned north all your life, only divine intervention will keep you from falling toward the north when you die, or from lying toward the north when it is all said and done.

So as you go through life, remember to think of God before . . .

- you grow too old to think clearly about serving God;

- your eyes grow cataracts, and you can't see well enough to read;

- your legs tremble from the exertion of walking from the couch to the bedroom;

- your shoulders stoop;

---

[3] At least one translation starts into 12:1 by saying "So, remember." Albert Barnes in his book *Notes on the Bible* suggests that it should read "And remember." The conjunction is not given in the Hebrew but can easily be understood.

Searching for Meaning

- your teeth can no longer chew your food properly;
- your eyes grow dim, and you can no longer find your way;
- the door to life's opportunities closes, and the sound of work fades from your life;
- your hearing fades, and you can no longer hear the chirping of the birds;
- you are afraid to walk alone because you might trip and fall;
- your hair grows white (or falls out) from age;
- you have no energy or desire left for the things you once loved to do or eat;
- the silver cord is cut, the golden bowl is broken, or the pitcher is shattered, and the pulley for drawing water from the well is broken; when mourners walk the streets to go to your funeral, and your body returns to the dust it was created from;
- God takes back the spirit of life which today still makes it possible for you to connect with Him.

It's a disquieting list. But unless God intervenes and you die an untimely death, this could be a description of you in your old age. Verse 6 adds some cryptic thoughts that seem to apply to the failure of bodily functions. I think you can easily fit adult diapers and catheters and feeding tubes and oxygen masks into this verse. This is reality for many older people.

Think how this would be. Do you really think this would be the ideal time to get right with God and repent of past actions? A friend of mine, who has now passed on, told me that he learned during a hospital experience that you had better not expect to be able to do a lot of repenting on your deathbed.

You will have enough questions and struggles when you are old without adding a careless youth and middle age to the equation. So face life realistically and serve God while you can. Then He will be with you when the "evil days draw nigh."

Futility Sets In (12:8)

Solomon worried a lot about the vanity and futility of a meaningless life. If you think life is futile now, wait until you face what we just looked at in the last section. I think Solomon learned in his old age what vanity is really all about.

> Vanity of vanities, saith the preacher; all is vanity. (Eccles. 12:8)

Vanity and futility come from losing touch with God or never finding Him in the first place. Vanity and futility also come from not being able to find Him when you finally realize how much you need Him.

What could be worse than God coming to you in your old age and telling you, "You didn't heed my warnings, and it's too late to change the consequences? You are now on your own."

Thankfully, that's not God's way, and at times people have found Him on their deathbeds or in their old age. But finding God at the last moment is not always possible. Don't take the chance.

A lifetime of futility is one thing. An eternity of futility is something totally different.

FOR DISCUSSION

Read Ecclesiastes 11:9–12:8

Prelude

When you are young, old age seems far away. When you are old, you wonder where all the time went and why you didn't get more done than you did. It happens to all of us, and it happened to Solomon.

1. Solomon describes old age as "the evil days." Why is this a fitting description? Does old age have to be like this?

Remember . . .

Memories can be good or bad. We can somewhat determine our memories by the life we choose to live. But when memories are made, they can't be undone.

2. If you are young, read this section to an older person and ask them what they think.

3. Why is being young a blessing? How can we turn it into a curse?

4. Dealing with the repercussions of past mistakes is not a happy task. But in what ways might it be a blessing in disguise if you are forced to do so?

Before . . .

Many people look forward to retirement. They look forward to days of playing golf and traveling, just relaxing and enjoying life. It's going to be a real utopia! Or will it?

5. We could summarize 12:1-6 as saying, "Remember God before you are old, and can't." Why is that such a chilling thought? Is it really true? Explain your answer.

6. Think carefully about the description of old age in this passage. Why is it unrealistic to expect to make major changes in your life when you are old?

7. Do your introspection now while you can still do something about your life. What are the things you would still like to do for God or change in your life before you die?

Futility Sets In

Solomon really didn't know the meaning of vanity and futility until he got old.

8. What is the major cause of people thinking life has no meaning or is full of vanity?

9. When God goes missing in your life, who got off the train, you or God? How can you reconnect?

10. Do you think God ever tells people, "You are now on your own"?

Fear God and Keep His Commandments

18

I have set before you life and death, blessing and cursing: therefore choose life, that both thou and thy seed may live: That thou mayest love the LORD thy God, and that thou mayest obey his voice, and that thou mayest cleave unto him: for he is thy life, and the length of thy days. Deuteronomy 30:19, 20

Prelude

Solomon laid down his pen. He was finished. His final work was accomplished.

He had given the responsibility of running the kingdom to Rehoboam, his son, some months ago. Since then, he had spent much of his time reading and thinking. He had done a lot of reminiscing, thinking over his past and sorting out everything that had happened. He knew he had made many mistakes. He also knew that the increasing troubles he and the kingdom had faced in the last several years were his own fault.

Even worse, he knew, from what the prophet had told him, that his son would also face repercussions. To protect him, he had tried to find and get rid of Jeroboam, but had failed.

"Maybe I should have told Rehoboam about the prophecy that Jeroboam would take ten of Israel's tribes away from him." He shook his head broodingly. "I guess he'll find it out for himself. I've tried to help him get ready, but he

thinks he can do so much better than I did. He'll have to learn the hard way."

He called for his servant, who came running. "I want to go to bed," he said, his voice shaking. He gathered together the loose scraps of parchment, some of which were covered with a somewhat shaky script. "Give these to my scribes," he told the servant. "They will know what to do. But first help me to my bed."

He paused for a moment at the door. The servant saw him glance around the room, as if saying goodbye.

Wisdom Should Be Shared (12:9-12)

Wisdom is of little value unless we share it. Solomon went to great effort to share his wisdom with his people. He collected proverbs written by others, he wrote proverbs of his own, and he apparently adapted the proverbs collected by others. Like any good writer, he wrestled with words. Some words say what you want, and others don't. Solomon wanted accurate words, words of truth that would portray truth to the people who read them.

If you read Proverbs, which was mostly his work, you will see the results of his efforts. He understood human nature, and he gave good advice about dealing with the situations life tends to bring with it.

The words of the wise can hurt at times. For instance, the NLT renders verse 11 like this: "The words of the wise are like cattle prods—painful but helpful. Their collected sayings are like a nail-studded stick with which a shepherd drives the sheep." Often, we reject wise counsel because it hurts, and we don't like to be hurt. Or it offends us, and we don't like that either. But can we look past the hurt and offense and take wise counsel to heart? If Solomon had taken more counsel from his wise men, he would have been wiser himself. After Solomon's death, Rehoboam's counselors tried to advise him of the right course of action, but he rejected their advice. I wonder if he had seen his father do the same.

Counsel should be given carefully and only when necessary. I have seen people who seem to feel obligated to share their "wisdom" very freely. Usually, people will listen more readily to the person who has fewer words of advice.

I don't think we should deliberately trample on toes when we give counsel. It isn't the harshness or intensity of our counsel that makes it effective. Kindness generally goes much deeper than harshness. You can usually tell if someone is giving you counsel out of genuine concern or just because he feels superior. The latter can be hard to handle gracefully.

However, wisdom is only a benefit when it is shared. I think it is important for older brethren in the church who have experience to be willing to share what they have learned. Share it kindly, share it when it is appropriate, and pray before you share it. But share it.

A friend of mine was a very sour young man in his youth. He looked like a thundercloud about to burst. When he walked into church, you got out of the way. But one day an older brother took him aside and told him quite frankly what he thought of his attitude. He informed him that with an attitude like his, he might as well stay home from church. I didn't hear the exchange, but knowing the young man as I did, and seeing what became of it, I suspect the older brother was *very* frank with him.

I still remember the next time I saw him. The difference was so obvious that I really wondered what had taken place.

I doubt that this older brother enjoyed doing what he did. He just saw a need and did it. I can think of all kinds of excuses that I would

> [9]And moreover, because the preacher was wise, he still taught the people knowledge; yea, he gave good heed, and sought out, and set in order many proverbs. [10]The preacher sought to find out acceptable words: and that which was written was upright, even words of truth. [11]The words of the wise are as goads, and as nails fastened by the masters of assemblies, which are given from one shepherd. [12]And further, by these, my son, be admonished: of making many books there is no end; and much study is a weariness of the flesh. (Eccles. 12:9-12)

likely give before I did something like that. Controversy isn't pleasant, and we try to avoid it whenever possible. Because of this, parents may hesitate to give their children good advice because they are afraid they will offend them. And ministers may be afraid to give wise counsel in their preaching for fear it will make them unpopular.

But wisdom doesn't help others unless we are willing to share it.

I'd like to emphasize one thing, however. Advice doesn't usually work well if we force the opportunity to give it. I think many times God will open up good opportunities for us to share. For instance, I remember a situation where I felt burdened to share some advice with another brother, but waited for God's timing. Then one day, during a conversation with him, he asked about the very situation I was burdened about. We had a good conversation about it, and I was glad I had waited for God's opportunity.

Another time I was feeling a bit upset about a situation and dived into it on my own accord. I would have been better off staying in bed that morning, because I just made a mess of the situation.

The final word of advice Solomon passes on is as interesting as it is unique. Of making many books there is no end, and much study is a weariness to the flesh. Advice means more if the person giving the advice knows what he is talking about. That was certainly true in this case.

Any person who does a lot of studying—such as a minister, a teacher, or an author—knows that it can become wearisome. I suspect this was Solomon's last book, though I have no proof of it. But everyone reading this last part of Ecclesiastes knows that Solomon knew what it meant to study and study, and study some more.

But I think his unspoken point in this verse is important: Be sure you know what you are talking about when you try to give advice. If you don't, you are better off just telling a person that you are praying for him and let God use someone else.

Wisdom is seldom useful unless it is practiced. A certain doctor who weighed about four hundred pounds used to lecture his overweight patients about their eating. "Don't do as I do, do as I say!" he told them. Somehow, I doubt if his lectures helped much. But one day he went on a diet. He also started to exercise regularly. And in a year's time, he lost over a hundred pounds.

Now he could bounce into an examination room and tell a patient, "Hey, you can lose weight! It's not so hard. I did!" His advice and encouragement meant something because he had "been there."

I don't know if Solomon did that. His track record in 1 Kings is tarnished. It doesn't work to tell someone to fear God and keep His commandments, then accompany your wife over the hill to worship her pagan god in a temple you built for her. I have laid out the possibility in this book that Solomon wrote Ecclesiastes after he turned around his own life. The Bible doesn't say whether he did that or not. I enjoy Ecclesiastes and it touches my heart, but it would mean just a little more if I knew for sure that it wasn't just an intellectual exposition of how you and I should live.

Keep that in mind when you try to tell other people how they should live.

Wisdom Is a Choice (12:13, 14)

Let's look at Solomon's conclusion. After all the twists and turns we have taken in this book, the conclusion seems quite simple.

Fear God and keep His commandments.

Why? He gives two reasons. First, it is the duty of man to do this.[1] And second, judgment is coming and God will examine your every act, whether good or bad. It doesn't matter whether other people have seen it or not. So, does that mean we make a list of everything God wants us to do or not do, and then do everything in our power to follow that list?

No, not really. Many people do that, however, because they seem to think following a list would be easier than serving God from the heart. That is why legalism is so common. But life isn't just a set of rules. Let's

---

[1] The word *duty* is a problem for translators. It is missing in the Hebrew text, yet something is needed for the clause to make sense. Most versions insert *duty* in this passage. But, like Adam Clarke states, it isn't really a good word to describe our relationship with God.

look at this conclusion a little closer.

What does it mean to *fear God?* Serving God has always been a choice. It is a choice that has consequences, but the person who obeys the rules simply because of the consequences doesn't really understand what God wants.

When God first created man, it appears He wanted someone He could fellowship with. Someone who would be His friend and be loyal to Him. Yes, God made some rules, but He put them in place for man's protection, not to be a hardship.

God still looks for this kind of relationship with men and women. Fearing God goes much beyond being terrified of Him or scared that He will punish you if you take a misstep.

Yes, we realize God has power to punish and to bring to judgment those who do evil. But fearing God as followers of Christ goes beyond this. God wants us to reverence Him, to worship Him, and to walk with Him. As we seek to serve Him, He will live in our hearts and be our Guide. Through His Holy Spirit He will teach us His will and give us power to live for Him.

We've already introduced what it means to *keep His commandments.* No matter how hard you try, you can never be perfect enough or obedient enough to work your way into heaven. Jesus said in the New Testament that the greatest of the commandments was to "Love the Lord thy God with all thy heart." The second commandment was similar—"Love thy neighbor as thyself." On these two commandments, He said, hang all the law and the prophets.[2] In other words, these two commandments summarize all of God's laws.

Love is one of those things you can't fake. God knows your heart. He

> [13]Let us hear the conclusion of the whole matter: Fear God, and keep his commandments: for this is the whole duty of man. [14]For God shall bring every work into judgment, with every secret thing, whether it be good, or whether it be evil. (Eccles. 12:13, 14)

---

[2] See Matthew 22:36-40, etc.

Searching for Meaning

knows what you really desire. Love is also something we can't truly have until God puts it into our heart. So we see that opening our heart to God is the only way to really fear Him and keep His commandments.

Serving God and living for Him is what life is all about. It is the only life worth living—the best life. I don't know if Solomon understood this or not. Maybe the Holy Spirit just revealed the words to him, and he wrote them down.

I hope he did understand. I hope you do too.

———

The picture is finished. This passage added the final brushstrokes. Or to use our other analogy, Solomon had found all the pieces of his jigsaw puzzle. He had sorted out and discarded any unneeded pieces. He had reached his conclusion—his climax, as it were—and there was nothing more to say.

I wonder, did he look back over this work and feel he had accomplished what he was after? Or did he feel as if he had done his best, but it wasn't quite what he had expected? That will be our feeling too if we're looking for meaning in life that promotes personal honor. If our goal is to honor God, however, the conclusion is the starting point we were looking for. As we recognize who God is and yield to His will, He can lead us into a deeper relationship with Him.

Ecclesiastes is a one-of-a-kind work of art. It is somewhat different from the rest of the Bible. It is very much a "treasure in an earthen vessel," and clearly reveals Solomon's personal struggles, as well as his often faulty understanding. But aren't we all works in progress? Just like Solomon, we are imperfect people and tend to see the world and life from an imperfect perspective. For that reason, we should be able to relate to Ecclesiastes, because it doesn't just reveal to us what Solomon was like. It also reveals what we are like.

Today we live in a new dispensation. We can experience forgiveness of sins and can have the power of the Holy Spirit living within us. And yet, if we are honest, we sense that God still has many things to teach us. Like Solomon, we find ourselves struggling to understand the complexities and the stresses of everyday life. We see that we have often made a crooked path, but we also see that God is teaching us and is leading us onward. Solomon's frustrations at times mirror our own, and his victories as well.

Despite his failures, let's not look down on Solomon. His way of reasoning things out and doing things his own way was very human—and we are prone to the same. God, however, is inviting us to make a more noble choice. He wants us to serve Him and walk with Him. As we do this we can find meaning in life even if things don't make sense.

FOR DISCUSSION

Read: Ecclesiastes 12:9-14

Prelude

Part of old age is giving up things we took for granted. Things like our independence and our privacy. But no one can take our spiritual legacy from us. It is said that Queen Victoria said on her deathbed that she would give all her money for another ten minutes of life. Death will take our life, but it cannot touch our legacy.

1. What is your legacy?

Wisdom Should Be Shared

Sometimes people are afraid to share their wisdom because they are afraid people might think they are proud or stubborn or looking for attention. Don't let that stop you from doing what you can to make the world around you a better place.

2. Why is it important to know what you are talking about before you try to give advice? Why is the method we use when we give advice so important?

3. When is a wrong time to give advice? When is a good time? How can you know?

4. Why is it important that we know how to "practice what we preach" when we give advice? How did Solomon fail in this?

Wisdom Is a Choice

This is a fitting conclusion to Ecclesiastes. When we can't find meaning in life and when life doesn't make sense, we tend to blame God. Or the government. Or the church. Or our boss. Or our spouse. But especially we tend to blame God.

5. What does it mean to fear God?

6. Why is following a checklist of dos and don'ts such a shallow way to serve God? What does it lack?

7. What really is the answer to finding meaning in life?

8. How do both the book of Ecclesiastes and its author symbolize the problems of the church and Christians today?

Finishing the Equation

And Solomon slept with his fathers, and was buried in the city of David his father: and Rehoboam his son reigned in his stead. 1 Kings 11:43

Prelude

One morning, some days after he had finished his writing, Solomon lacked the strength to get out of bed. Everyone knew the end was near. His closest friends were the servants and guards who had served him for years. One by one they found excuses to slip into his room to say goodbye.

Many of his wives had already died. Naamah had died some years before, or she might have come to say goodbye, though Solomon hadn't said goodbye to her before she died. The Egyptian princess, in her own way, had always admired Solomon, but she too was gone. Solomon had said goodbye to her. He missed her more than most of his wives because she had intruded into his life more than any of the others. None of his women who still lived cared enough to come and see him. They were too worried about their own future to think about Solomon. The matron did come and seemed strangely moved, leaving with tears running down her cheeks.

Solomon seemed troubled and in a world of his own. He scarcely saw the friends who gathered around him. But eventually he roused himself enough to whisper to his servant, "Please find the prophet and bring him here."

The servant said a few words to a guard at the door. The guard left, almost running. He returned about an hour later with the young man who had stood in Solomon's audience chamber several years earlier. The prophet came to his bedside slowly and with bent head.

"You wanted me, sir?" His voice was quiet, but fearless.

The king opened his eyes and whispered, "Tell me, will God accept me despite my foolish mistakes?"

The prophet showed emotion for the first time. He had apparently anticipated the king's question, and his voice broke a little as he answered, "Sir, I do not know. God has hidden it from me."

The room was quiet, and the king spoke no more.

"It is very dangerous to go into eternity with possibilities which one has oneself prevented from becoming realities. A possibility is a hint from God. One must follow it." (Soren Kierkegaard)

Further Thoughts About Solomon

A lot of people have asked the question: Was Solomon ready to die? The answers have varied all the way from "Of course he was" to "No, he wasn't." Probably most of us would answer, "I don't know." It isn't up to me to decide that, and any decision I made would mean nothing on the judgment day.

I suspect that the "of-course-he-was" people like to think that the grace of God will see you through even if you did some things that God didn't like. Maybe they have "weaknesses" in their own lives that they hope God will overlook as well.

On the other hand, the "no-he-wasn't" folks are possibly the kind who stand firm on the fact that God expects us to be perfect and will never let sin enter heaven. But have they reached that level themselves? Most would squirm a bit if you asked them that question. I'm not saying they are wrong. I'm just noting that even such people have struggles that don't quite seem to fit the formula they promote.

I'm willing to leave the question in God's hands.

Further Thoughts About Ecclesiastes

As I said before, Ecclesiastes reveals a lot about Solomon, but it reveals just as much about you and me. We really aren't much different than Solomon was, especially if we allow our carnal nature to direct us. Solomon loved many strange women. Can you honestly say you have never allowed such thoughts or desires in your heart? Solomon loved pleasure and material things. Maybe you have never lived an extravagant lifestyle quite like Solomon did. Yet in the eyes of most of the people in the world today, you are a very privileged and wealthy person.

Solomon didn't have Christ in his heart or the Holy Spirit in his heart to guide him, as we can have. If you act like Solomon today, as a professing Christian, you are in worse shape than he was. So allow the book of Ecclesiastes to be a mirror for you and find yourself in it.

We can't blame Solomon for having a limited understanding of what it takes to find meaning in life. The true answer for that didn't show up for almost another thousand years. However, if following his own conclusion at the end of Ecclesiastes—fear God and keep His commandments—had truly been Solomon's goal, think how much different his life could have been.

Some Old Testament believers knew more about relating to God than Solomon did. His father, David, had the Holy Spirit (see 1 Samuel 16:13), but this was not the norm in that era. Some of the prophets, like Elijah, probably had a similar experience. But it was much more common for the guidance of the Spirit to be given only in times of great need. According to 2 Timothy 3:16, all Scripture is given by inspiration of God, so we know that in some way the Holy Spirit oversaw what Solomon wrote in Ecclesiastes.

Since Solomon used observable data for the backbone of this book, he avoided the supernatural in most cases. That doesn't mean he didn't believe in the supernatural, or in eternity, but that wasn't his focus. His focus was finding meaning in life when life seemed meaningless. In the end, he seemed to conclude that the meaninglessness was more in his perspective of life than in the reality. It also had more to do with the fact that he had lost sight of God than it did with God distancing Himself from him. However, with the book written in this way, an unconverted or depressed person can pick up the book and identify with it. *Hey, that's exactly how I feel. My life is meaningless too.* But as he continues reading, Solomon starts to enter avenues that will make an intelligent person stop and think. *Hmm. That's true too. Maybe there are some simple pleasures in life that I've been overlooking.* Hopefully, he'll follow Solomon all the way to the end. *Wow, I'd better get my house in order. God is real and is keeping track of my life.*

But every Bible should have a note at the end of Ecclesiastes that says, "To Be Continued—See Matthew 12:42." The end of the story is found in the New Testament.

A Greater (Person) Than Solomon

The scribes and Pharisees came to Jesus one day and asked Him for a sign that would prove that He was who He claimed to be. They had seen many signs already, but they were not satisfied. Jesus was somewhat exasperated at them and told them that other people in history had believed with fewer signs than He had already given them (I'm reading between the lines a little here). Referring to the Queen of Sheba, He told them, "The queen of the south shall rise up in the judgment with this generation, and shall condemn it: for she came from the uttermost parts of the earth to hear the wisdom of Solomon; and, behold, a greater than Solomon is here."[1]

Solomon was a brilliant thinker. He noticed that life of itself was

---

[1] You can read this in context in Matthew 12:38-42.

meaningless. In Ecclesiastes, he went to great lengths to prove this. He looked for a logical answer to this enigma, since he didn't believe that God would create anything that was truly meaningless. The universe had to be more than just a perpetual-motion machine that might crash at any time because a bearing went out. People had to be more than robots, blindly fulfilling a preprogrammed destiny. His conclusion, as I hinted earlier, was likely deflating to him. Really? Just fear God and obey Him? Just do that because He will judge everything you do?

Solomon's honest, philosophical examination of life eventually brought him to the right conclusion. But knowing the answer and living it are two different things. Man can never truly serve God by his own strength and reasoning. As Ecclesiastes clearly shows, intellectualism can never bridge the gap between us and God.

We could add other questions that Solomon didn't address. What if I don't have the spiritual strength to do what God commands? What if I don't know what God wants me to do? Job faced this when he cried out, "But how should man be just with God?" (Read Job 9 to get a complete context.) Later in the chapter, he laments that there was no mediator or arbitrator to stand between him and God. That was part of Solomon's problem too.

But God knew all about this. The "master plan" that Solomon was sure existed somewhere was centered on this need for someone to bridge the gap between man and God. I believe God had been working toward this solution ever since the fall of man. Even though man had sinned against Him, God took the first step toward reconciliation. In fact, He took the second step and the third step

> Then Job answered and said, I know it is so of a truth: but how should man be just with God? . . . .
> If I wash myself with snow water, and make my hands never so clean; Yet shalt thou plunge me in the ditch, and mine own clothes shall abhor me. For he is not a man, as I am, that I should answer him, and we should come together in judgment. Neither is there any daysman betwixt us that might lay his hand upon us both. Let him take his rod away from me, and let not his fear terrify me: Then would I speak, and not fear him; but it is not so with me. (Job 9:1, 2, 30-35)

and many more steps. Man was floundering and had no idea how to bridge the gap, but God was slowly but surely putting it all in place.

First He started putting more pressure on man to show him how far he had fallen. This started on a personal level with men like Enoch, Noah, and Abraham. Then He moved it to a national level, working through Moses to give His people the Law. The Law revealed God's moral expectations more clearly than anyone had ever known them before. Then God followed up with prophets who brought the Law down to a personal level. Prophets like Isaiah helped people to see into their own hearts and realize how wide the gap was between them and God.

Finally, almost abruptly, God stopped communicating altogether. For almost four hundred years, He said nothing. Then, when many thinking people had almost given up hope, God broke the silence by sending an angel to Zacharias, a priest who was offering incense in the temple. God followed up with another angel about six months later. This time the messenger went to Nazareth to a young unmarried woman named Mary.

Mary's Son, Jesus, was the answer—the Arbitrator and Mediator who would be the bridge that brought God and man back into fellowship. He was conceived by the power of the Holy Spirit rather than the seed of a man and was God in a human body. The waiting was over, and the angels shouted with joy over the rolling hills of Judea at the birth of Jesus. This was what eternity had been holding its breath for. This was the opening shot in the battle to restore the relationship between men and women and their God.

The wonders of the incarnation and the atonement are hard for us to grasp. And at the time Christ came, only a few people recognized that the great moment had come. But there were enough. On the day of Pentecost 120 people were waiting for the next step, the outpouring of the Holy Spirit on the believers. Before the day was over this little group had baptized three thousand people, and the move was on in earnest. Historians say that within fifty years, most of the world had been evangelized.

Meaning in Life

Solomon's questions had finally been answered. So had Job's. The two really had the same question, because you can't find meaning in life without bridging the gap between you and God. Job wanted someone who could put one hand on his shoulder and another on God's shoulder and bring them face to face. Jesus can do that if we let Him. Both Solomon and Job would have loved this answer had they been able to see it.

Do you realize how great a privilege you have? You can meet God face to face, as it were. Jesus will bridge the gap between you and God. You can find meaning in life. *Real meaning.* Meaning that all the world's riches and all the world's pretty women and all the world's natural and philosophical marvels could never begin to give you. Solomon proved that these things did not bring meaning to life. Jesus Christ came to offer that meaning to the poorest beggar on the planet.

Let us hear the conclusion of the whole matter: *Christ Jesus came into the world to save sinners; of whom I am chief* (1 Tim. 1:15).

FOR DISCUSSION

Prelude

Consider the quote from Kierkegaard at the end of the prelude. This is referring to the opportunities God has given us but which we have not taken advantage of.

1. What are some of the "possibilities" that God gives to His children? How might we prevent them from becoming realities? Why would this be dangerous?

Further Thoughts

I would suggest not wasting time over the question, "Was Solomon ready to die?" Instead, discuss what Ecclesiastes has taught you about yourself.

2. Why wasn't it possible for Solomon to get a complete answer to his questions about finding meaning in life?

3. According to Galatians 3:23-26, the Law was given to be a governess or guardian to keep God's children faithful until the day of Christ could come. How does Solomon's answer fit in with that concept?

4. Job's question in Job 9, "How can a man be just with God?" is an extension of Solomon's question. But Job didn't really get his questions answered either. When did God finally answer both Solomon's and Job's questions? How?

5. How did Jesus finally bridge the gap between man and God? How does this bring meaning to life that was missing before?

About the Author

Lester Bauman was born into an Old Order Mennonite home close to Kitchener, Ontario. Later his family joined a local conservative Mennonite church. As a young-married man, he taught for five years in several Christian schools. Later he worked for thirteen years out of a home office for Rod and Staff Publishers, Inc. as a writer and editor. During this time, he and his wife Marlene moved with their family from Ontario to Alberta, where they live presently. They have six children and eleven grandchildren, and are members of a local Western Fellowship Mennonite Church.

During his time with Rod and Staff, Lester wrote ten books, including *The True Christian* and *God and Uncle Dale,* both available from Christian Aid Ministries. He spent a number of years in Alberta working as an HR manager in a corporate setting. He now works for the Christian Aid Ministries billboard evangelism ministry out of a home office, doing content writing for their website, answering correspondence, and writing resource materials.

Lester has written several other books published by Christian Aid Ministries: *Sylvester's Journal* and *What Is the Bible?* He is also working on several other books as time allows.

You can contact Lester through his personal website at www.lbauman.ca or by email at lester.bauman@gmail.com. You may also write to him in care of Christian Aid Ministries, P.O. Box 360, Berlin, Ohio 44610.

About Christian Aid Ministries

Christian Aid Ministries was founded in 1981 as a nonprofit, tax-exempt 501(c)(3) organization. Its primary purpose is to provide a trustworthy and efficient channel for Amish, Mennonite, and other conservative Anabaptist groups and individuals to minister to physical and spiritual needs around the world. This is in response to the command to ". . . do good unto all men, especially unto them who are of the household of faith" (Galatians 6:10).

Each year, CAM supporters provide 15–20 million pounds of food, clothing, medicines, seeds, Bibles, Bible story books, and other Christian literature for needy people. Most of the aid goes to orphans and Christian families. Supporters' funds also help to clean up and rebuild for natural disaster victims, put up Gospel billboards in the U.S., support several church-planting efforts, operate two medical clinics, and provide resources for needy families to make their own living.

CAM's main purposes for providing aid are to help and encourage God's people and bring the Gospel to a lost and dying world.

CAM has staff, warehouses, and distribution networks in Romania, Moldova, Ukraine, Haiti, Nicaragua, Liberia, Israel, and Kenya. Aside from management, supervisory personnel, and bookkeeping operations, volunteers do most of the work at CAM locations. Each year, volunteers at our warehouses, field bases, Disaster Response Services projects, and other locations donate over 200,000 hours of work.

CAM's ultimate purpose is to glorify God and help enlarge His kingdom. ". . . whatsoever ye do, do all to the glory of God" (1 Corinthians 10:31).

The Way to God and Peace

We live in a world contaminated by sin. Sin is anything that goes against God's holy standards. When we do not follow the guidelines that God our Creator gave us, we are guilty of sin. Sin separates us from God, the source of life.

Since the time when the first man and woman, Adam and Eve, sinned in the Garden of Eden, sin has been universal. The Bible says that we all have "sinned and come short of the glory of God" (Romans 3:23). It also says that the natural consequence for that sin is eternal death, or punishment in an eternal hell: "Then when lust hath conceived, it bringeth forth sin: and sin, when it is finished, bringeth forth death" (James 1:15).

But we do not have to suffer eternal death in hell. God provided forgiveness for our sins through the death of His only Son, Jesus Christ. Because Jesus was perfect and without sin, He could die in our place.

"For God so loved the world that he gave his only begotten Son, that whosoever believeth in him should not perish, but have everlasting life" (John 3:16).

A sacrifice is something given to benefit someone else. It costs the giver greatly. Jesus was God's sacrifice. Jesus' death takes away the penalty of sin for all those who accept this sacrifice and truly repent of their sins. To repent of sins means to be truly sorry for and turn away from the things we have done that have violated God's standards (Acts 2:38; 3:19).

Jesus died, but He did not remain dead. After three days, God's Spirit miraculously raised Him to life again. God's Spirit does something similar in us. When we receive Jesus as our sacrifice and repent of our sins, our hearts are changed. We become spiritually alive! We develop new desires and attitudes (2 Corinthians 5:17). We begin to make choices that please God (1 John 3:9). If we do fail and commit sins, we can ask God for forgiveness. "If we confess our sins, he is faithful and just to forgive us our sins, and to cleanse us from all unrighteousness" (1 John 1:9).

Once our hearts have been changed, we want to continue growing spiritually. We will be happy to let Jesus be the Master of our lives and will want to become more like Him. To do this, we must meditate on God's Word and commune with God in prayer. We will testify to others of this change by being baptized and sharing the good news of God's victory over sin and death. Fellowship with a faithful group of believers will strengthen our walk with God (1 John 1:7).